GOLD AND THE

DOLLAR CRISIS

The Future of Convertibility

by ROBERT TRIFFIN

REVISED EDITION

NEW HAVEN AND LONDON

YALE UNIVERSITY PRESS

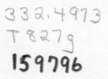

To my children:

NICKY
KERRY
ERIC

*who undoubtedly will, some years from now,
feel inordinately proud or amused, when dis-
covering this intrepid attempt of their father
to prophesy history and to deflect its course.*

Warning

Following a time-hallowed custom, the author regretfully warns the reader that the views expressed in this book do not necessarily reflect the opinions—if any—held by the official organizations with which he has been, or is now, associated.

Preface

THE MAIN BODY of this book reproduces, with only minor changes, the text of two articles published in March and June of 1959 in the *Banca Nazionale del Lavoro Quarterly Review*.

The first of these articles (Part One: Diagnosis) explains, in the broadest possible terms, the extraordinary success of the nineteenth-century system of international convertibility and the calamitous collapse of the late 1920's brave attempt to bring it back to life after World War I. It boldly tries to pry out of this musty record the lessons it may hold for us today and an indication of the main dangers facing the similar attempt at "reconstructing the past" launched some thirty years later during the 1958 Christmas weekend.

The second article (Part Two: Prescription) ventures, even more boldly, to outline the radical institutional reforms which might ward off these dangers by adapting to present-day needs and conditions a set of international monetary institutions which adjusted remarkably flexibly to their own, nineteenth-century, economic and political environment, but whose revival and survival today require far more than a mere digging-up and dusting-off of a dead body from its fifty-year-old grave.

These, needless to say, are formidably technical topics. To deal with them in simple, commonsense terms, would inevitably classify the author as a crackpot whose views deserve no more than a raising of eyebrows and a shrugging of the shoulders on the part of serious-minded people. I felt compelled, therefore, to meet the experts—and particularly those of the International Monetary Fund—on their own grounds, to counter their arguments, and to anticipate their objections. This makes unnecessarily forbidding reading for the layman. Yet, he too has a vital interest in these issues. It is he, indeed, who will ultimately decide their solution through his elected representatives in Congress and the Administration. I particularly welcomed, for this reason, the invitation of the Joint Economic Committee of Congress to present to them, on October 28 of last year, the main issues at stake and their relevance to the United States' economic position and policies.

vii

My oral statement to the Committee is reproduced verbatim in the introductory chapter of this book. The man in the street will probably discover there all that he wishes to know about the problem and my suggested solutions for it.[1]

I am very conscious of the danger of committing to a book—whose printing and publication will take months—a number of views which the fast-changing course of world events might soon render obsolete.[2] Some of the problems dealt with here may well have assumed a very different shape by the time this book reaches the reader. Thus, the liquidity crisis which caused so much concern in 1958 was temporarily relieved last year for Western Europe, but at the cost of a huge deterioration in the reserve position of the United States and of a further aggravation in the position of most underdeveloped countries.

1. Those readers who, on the contrary, wish for further historical background and theoretical analysis, may consult my book on *Europe and the Money Muddle* (Yale University Press, 1957), and particularly Chapter 1 (The World Dollar Shortage), Chapter 3 (The Failure of the International Currency Plans: 1944–47), Chapter 6 (Current Approaches to Convertibility), Chapter 7 (Toward Viable Convertibility), and Chapter 8 (Current Prospects and Conclusions: The Tasks Ahead).

2. May I be permitted to hide modestly in a footnote the immodest claim of having been rather lucky in some previous excursions of this sort?

The proposals for a multilateralization of bilateral payments agreements in Europe which I vainly tried to press upon the International Monetary Fund in 1947, 1948, and 1949 were finally taken over by the European Cooperation Administration and developed into the European Payments Union Agreement in 1950. The spectacular success of EPU in the liberalization of European trade and payments, and in paving the way for the gradual restoration of convertibility itself, has finally stilled the strenuous objections raised at that time by most of my academic colleagues, and by many of our high officials and experts in Washington, against the formation of an "autarkic, high-cost, soft currency area sheltering itself by discrimination from world-wide competition."

In the winter of 1953–54, I was asked by the Council of Economic Advisers to organize an inter-agency committee aimed at developing concrete recommendations about the measures which we should take to alleviate the probable impact of the U.S. recession on the world dollar position. The conclusion of our committee that a moderate recession would merely slow down—but not reverse—the current accumulation of gold and dollar holdings by foreign countries was greeted mostly with sarcasm at the time by technicians long steeped in dollar shortage theories. Yet, it was soon confirmed by the facts of the case.

Finally, the fears which I expressed more than three years ago, in *Europe and the Money Muddle*, about a forthcoming "dollar glut" were derided by most reviewers of my book, whose untimely appearance in print happened to coincide with a brief renewal of some dollar difficulties abroad in connection with the Suez crisis. Those fears unfortunately forecast accurately a situation which has now become a matter of common, and grave concern, here and abroad.

Yet, I am confident that the basic themes of this book will remain valid for policy-makers for a long time to come. Gold production is unlikely to increase sufficiently in the foreseeable future to provide an adequate supply of liquidity to an expanding world economy; and the haphazard use of national currency holdings as a supplementary form of reserve accumulation cannot but undermine, more and more dangerously as time goes on, the key currencies used for this purpose and, by way of consequence, the world monetary superstructure erected upon them.

Whether or not the concrete proposals developed here to meet these problems have any chance to be negotiated in time to avoid a major crisis in the international monetary system, is an entirely different matter which history alone can, and will, answer.

New Haven   R. T.
Halloween 1959

PREFACE TO THE PAPERBOUND EDITION

THE APPEARANCE of the first edition of this book on the eve of the dollar crisis in the fall of 1960 proved as timely as the publication of *Europe and the Money Muddle* in the middle of the Suez crisis had been untimely.

Except for minor revisions in some of the estimates presented in Table 14, and the correction of three inconsequential misprints, no alterations have been made in Parts One and Two of the original edition.

The previous POSTSCRIPT: INITIAL REACTIONS, OFFICIAL AND OTHER, however, has been considerably condensed in order to make room for a brief narrative of the events which have taken place since the original manuscript went to press. It has therefore been retitled: TO BRING UP TO DATE AN UNFINISHED STORY.

May I express, in closing, my deep appreciation to Mrs. Carol Ransley for her speedy and perfect typing of my manuscript, and to Chester Kerr, Mrs. Marian Ash, and the whole Yale University Press, for their constant prodding and encouragement, as well as for a most competent editing, publishing, and distributing job.

New Haven   R. T.
Inauguration Day 1961

Contents

Tables

Postscript Tables

Charts

BY WAY OF INTRODUCTION

Statement to the Joint Economic
Committee of the 87th Congress
(Washington, October 28, 1959)

The International Monetary Position

and Policy of the United States

I

1. Let me first apologize for being unable to offer you today more than a very narrow contribution to the broad and fundamental policy issues debated by your Committee. The time at my disposal was extremely short, and my only field of competence—if any—lies in the area of international monetary policy, rather than in the field of domestic economic policies which is the main concern of this inquiry.

I am very much afraid, however, that the evolution of the last ten years has now brought us to a point where these issues have become inextricably tangled with one another, and where we can no longer afford to ignore the impact of our internal policies upon our external position, and vice versa. We have certainly licked that famous, supposedly permanent and untractable dollar shortage which dominated for more than ten years economic thinking and policy here and abroad. I only pray to God that none of my bright colleagues come up tomorrow with an opposite, and equally absurd, theory of a permanent and untractable dollar glut. Before placing before you a number of disturbing facts and ominous danger signals, let me affirm in no uncertain terms that I do not believe for a minute that our present difficulties are either permanent or untractable. The strength and resiliency of our economy and of our policies make it certain that they can, and that they will, be solved.

2. I have dealt rather briefly and inadequately, in my written statement, with the alarming deterioration in our balance of payments

Table 1
Balance of Payments of the United States, 1952-1959
(Annual rates, in billions of dollars)

	With the World			With Western Europe			With the Rest of the World		
	1952-57	1958	January-June 1959[1]	1952-57	1958	January-June 1959	1952-57	1958	January-June 1959[2]
1. Balance on Goods, Services, and Ordinary Transfers	2.1	1.5	-1.2	0.1	-0.8	-2.3	2.0	.4	1.1
2. Net Exports of U.S. Capital and Economic Aid	3.9	5.4	3.9[3]	1.2	0.8	0.8	2.8	4.7	3.7[3]
A. Private	1.8	2.8	2.0	0.3	0.4	0.6	1.5	2.4	1.4
B. Official	2.2	2.6	2.4[3]	0.9	0.4	0.2	1.3	2.2	2.2[3]
3. Overall Balance (1-2), offset by:	-1.8	-3.9	-5.0	-1.1	-1.6	-3.1	-0.7	-2.3	-2.0
A. Errors, Omissions and Triangular Settlements	-0.5	-0.4	-0.8	—	1.3	-0.3	-0.5	-1.7	-0.5
B. Inflow (−) of Long Term Foreign Capital	-0.3	—	-0.5	-0.2	—	-0.4	-0.1	—	-0.1
C. Gold Sales and Increases in Foreign Dollar Holdings (−)	-1.1	-3.4	-3.7[3]	-0.9	-2.9	-2.4	-0.2	-0.5	-1.3[3]
(i) Dollar Holdings	-1.1	-1.1	-2.7[3]	-0.7	-0.6	-1.7	-0.3	-0.6	-1.1[3]
(ii) Gold Sales	—	-2.3	-1.0[3]	-0.2	-2.3	-0.7	0.2	0.1	-0.3[3]
Related Information									
4. Military Transactions									
A. Exports under grants	2.9	2.5	1.9	2.2	1.5	1.2	0.7	1.1	0.7
B. Expenditures Abroad	2.7	3.4	3.2	1.4	1.9	1.8	1.3	1.6	1.4
5. Increase in Foreign Gold and Dollar Holdings:	1.6	4.3	4.7[3]	1.3	3.7	3.0	0.3	0.6	1.7[3]
A. From Estimated U.S. Transactions	1.1	3.4	3.7[3]	0.9	1.6	2.7	0.2	1.8	1.0[3]
B. Other	0.5	0.9	1.0	0.4	2.1	0.3	0.1	-1.2	0.7

Source: Survey of Current Business

Footnotes: 1. Seasonally adjusted, except items 4 and 5b and breakdown of item 2.

2. Figures in this column were calculated by subtracting seasonally *unadjusted* estimates for Western Europe from seasonally *adjusted* estimates for the world. This has the effect of ascribing to transactions with the rest of the world only the total of these adjustments.

3. Excluding from item 2B gold ($344 millions) and currency ($1,031 millions) subscriptions to the increase of the IMF capital, and the impact of these operations on items 3C, 5 and 5A.

CHART I

Balance of Payments of the United States, 1949–1959
(billions of dollars)

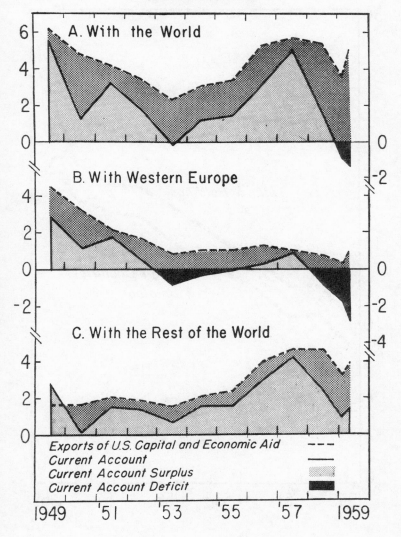

A. With the World

B. With Western Europe

C. With the Rest of the World

Exports of U.S. Capital and Economic Aid
Current Account
Current Account Surplus
Current Account Deficit

1949   '51   '53   '55   '57   1959

CHART II

U.S. Gold and Foreign Dollar Holdings, 1949–1959
(billions of dollars)

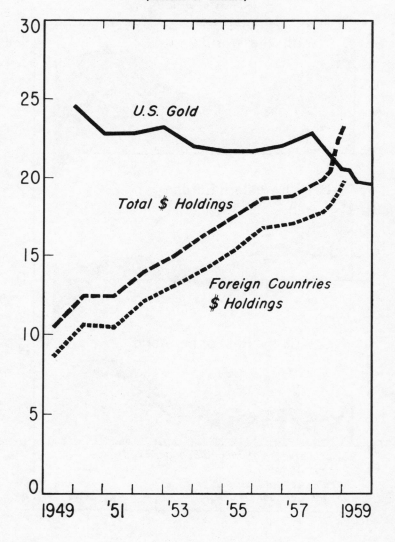

TABLE 2
World Monetary Gold and Dollar Holdings, 1949-1959
(in millions of U.S. dollars)

	Monetary Gold[1]				Dollar Holdings			Gold and Dollar Holdings		
	Total	United States	Foreign Countries	International Institutions	Total	Foreign Countries	International Institutions	United States[2]	Foreign Countries	International Institutions
	(a = b + c + d)	(b)	(c)	(d)	(e = f + g)	(f)	(g)	(h = b − f)	(i = c + f)	(j = d + g)
End of:										
1949	35,055	24,563	9,041	1,451	8,226	6,409	1,817	18,154	15,450	3,268
1950	35,498	22,820	11,184	1,494	10,197	8,393	1,804	14,427	19,577	3,298
1951	35,664	22,873	11,261	1,530	10,173	8,271	1,902	14,602	19,532	3,432
1952	35,968	23,252	11,024	1,692	11,719	9,864	1,855	13,388	20,888	3,547
1953	36,396	22,091	12,603	1,702	12,739	10,825	1,914	11,266	23,428	3,616
1954	37,056	21,793	13,523	1,740	14,019	11,895	2,124	9,898	25,418	3,864
1955	37,716	21,753	14,155	1,808	15,230	13,028	2,202	8,725	27,183	4,010
1956	38,246	22,058	14,496	1 692	16,433	14,590	1,843	7,468	29,086	3,535
1957	38,960	22,857	14,923	1,180	16,600	14,861	1,739	7,996	29,784	2,919
1958	39,851	20,582	17,937	1,332	17,637	15,598	2,039	4,984	33,535	3,371
1959:										
March	40,073	20,486	18,216	1,371	18,250	16,052	2,199	4,434	34,268	3,570
June	40,332	19,746	18,677	1,909	20,055	16,776	3,279	2,970	35,453	5,188
Change:										
1950-58	+4,796	−3,981	+8,896	−119	+9,411	+9,189	+222	−13,270	+18,085	+103

Source: Federal Reserve Bulletin.

Footnotes: 1. Gold estimates are obtained residually by deducting dollar holdings from gold and dollar holdings.
2. Excess of U.S. gold stock over dollar holdings of foreign countries only, but not of international institutions.

and the doubts which this may raise about whether or not we are pricing ourselves out of the world markets. This topic, however, has already been covered at great length by other and more qualified speakers, and I think you will prefer to save time by leaving it out of my oral presentation.

Let me merely comment very briefly on a highly simplified chart which I am now placing before you. Each portion of this chart shows:

a) in dotted lines, our total exports of U.S. capital and economic aid;

b) in full lines, our current account balance;
   (i) fine screen showing surpluses;
   (ii) solid black surfaces showing deficits;

c) in coarse screen, the excess of our capital exports and economic aid over our current account surpluses.

Three major observations emerge from this chart:

a) The pronounced downward trend of our current account with Western Europe—interrupted only by the height of the European boom and the Suez crisis—strongly supports other evidence pointing to the persistent and growing deterioration in our competitive position vis-à-vis this area.

b) This is veiled in the evolution of our current account with the world at large—in the top portion of the chart—by the growing surpluses which we enjoyed until last year with the rest of the world—as shown in the bottom part of the chart. These surpluses with the rest of the world seem, however, to be closely associated with the level of the financing made available to these countries by our own exports of capital and economic aid. The two lines of this portion of the Chart are nearly parallel to one another. Their tendency to grow somewhat further apart in 1958 and 1959 might possibly be related again to the deterioration of our competitive position vis-à-vis Western Europe, other countries finding it more economic to use their financial resources to buy in Europe rather than here.

c) Finally, our overall exports of capital and economic aid have been relatively sustained throughout this whole period of ten years, at levels considerably in excess of our current account surpluses. This gap has been financed mostly by a persistent deterioration of our net external reserve and liquidity position, through the gold losses and increasing short term indebtedness abroad depicted in Chart II, which I am now bringing before you.

3. I have no really original advice to offer regarding the policies which we should follow to plug these persistent and growing deficits in our overall payments balance.

I mention in my written statement some obvious reasons—shared by many other witnesses who have appeared before this Committee— for doubting both the effectiveness and the desirability of some remedies which seem to me as dangerous ultimately as they are plausible at first view. I have in mind any recommendations for drastic cuts in our capital exports or economic aid to the underdeveloped countries, for the tying of such loans or aid to purchases in the United States, and—even worse—for a relapse into protectionist policies and import restrictions.

Our main problem is not to retrench, but to advance, not to cut our imports and our capital contribution to economic development abroad, but to restore our exports to levels sufficient to enable us to pursue in the future, on a sounder and more durable basis, policies which have abundantly proved their worth and which are indispensable both to our own internal growth and to the maintenance of our economic and political position in the world of tomorrow.

After saying what we should *not* do, let me say what I think we *should* do.

We must, first of all, strengthen, or recover, our competitiveness in world trade, by arresting creeping inflation here, while stepping up our rates of growth and productivity by appropriate investments in research and technology.

We should, secondly, continue to press more and more vigorously for the elimination of remaining discrimination on dollar goods and the further reduction of other obstacles to trade and payments by foreign countries, and particularly by prosperous Europe.

Thirdly, the liberalization of foreign obstacles to American exports should stimulate our own producers to devote more attention than they do now to prospecting foreign markets and expanding their sales abroad.

Fourthly, we should do everything to prod European countries to assume their fair share of development financing abroad, particularly through multilateral assistance programs rather than through bilateral, tied loan, procedures.

Last but not least, the current relaxation of world tensions may possibly enable us to reduce the terrifying and disproportionate defense burdens—internal as well as external—which probably account, more than any other single factor, for the revolutionary shift which has taken place in the international dollar balance from prewar to postwar days. This, however, is only a hope yet, and one about which I feel totally incompetent to hazard any guess or suggestion. If it were to be disappointed once more, we should probably re-examine with our allies the problem of a fair allocation of our joint defense costs.

II

1. All that I have said so far, and much more which I have left unsaid, has become by now trite and familiar to the members of this Committee. Let me, therefore, center my testimony on two other, closely interrelated, problems on which I feel—rightly or wrongly— that I have something to say that will be both new and constructive for your Committee.

Even the most successful readjustment of our overall balance of payments will leave in its wake two major problems, of vital concern not only to us, but to the rest of the world as well. Both have to do with the functioning of international monetary convertibility in an expanding world economy. The satisfactory functioning of such a system necessarily requires an expanding pool of world monetary reserves and international liquidity, to bridge temporary and unavoidable fluctuations in each country's external receipts and payments. Such fluctuations would, otherwise, force widespread and recurrent recourses to deflation, currency devaluation or trade and exchange restrictions.

Gold has long ceased to provide more than a fraction of the minimum requirements for the preservation of adequate reserve and liquidity levels. Most—although not all—countries, however, have shown themselves willing to accumulate a substantial portion of their monetary reserves in the form of foreign exchange—primarily sterling and dollar balances—alongside of gold itself. The trouble with this solution—known as the "gold exchange standard"—is that it is bound to undermine, more and more dangerously as time goes on, the international liquidity position of the currencies used as reserves by other countries and, by way of consequence, to impart an increasing vulnerability to the world monetary superstructure built upon these so-called "key currencies." Indeed, the additions to international liquidity made possible by the system are entirely dependent upon the willingness of the key currency countries to allow their own net reserve position to deteriorate, by letting their short term liabilities to foreigners grow persistently and indefinitely at a faster pace than their own gold assets.

I recall, in my written statement, how this led, in 1931, to the devaluation of the pound sterling, to the collapse of the international gold exchange standard, and to the consequent aggravation of the world depression.

Circumstances are undoubtedly different today. Yet two problems are inescapable.

The first is that the elimination of our overall balance of payments deficits would, by definition, put an end to the constant deterioration of our monetary reserves and deprive thereby the rest of the world of the major source by far—two thirds to three fourths—from which the international liquidity requirements of an expanding world economy have been met in recent years, in the face of a totally inadequate supply of monetary gold.

The second is that the huge legacy of short term foreign indebtedness already inherited by us from the past is likely to place a heavy handicap on sound policies for economic growth and stability in this country. Refugee capital has flown here in large amounts after the second world war, as it had flown to London after the first world war. Some of it may return home, as currency conditions become definitely stabilized in Europe, just as it left London in the late 1920's. Our huge gold losses of last year were due in part to such a repatriation of foreign capital at a time when interest rates had fallen here well below the rates available in Europe. They have been slowed down this year by an extremely sharp rise of interest rates in this country, prompted by our domestic concern about creeping inflation. In this case, external and internal interest rate policy criteria happily coincided, but they may diverge tomorrow. If and when we feel reassured about our internal price and cost trends we may wish to ease credit and lower interest rates in order to spur our laggard rate of economic growth in comparison not only with Russia, but with Europe as well. We may then be caught, however, exactly as the

British were in the 1920's, between these legitimate and essential
policy objectives and the need to retain short term funds here in
order to avoid excessive gold losses.

I cannot resist quoting an incisive remark of Santayana, most aptly
used by the Managing Director of the International Monetary Fund
in several of his recent speeches: "Those who do not remember the
past will be condemned to repeat it."

2.   Can we find a way out of the double dilemma which I have just
mentioned? I think we can. The problem lies in both cases, with the
absurdities associated with the use of *national* currencies as *international* reserves. It can be met, most directly and simply, by the
internationalization of the foreign exchange component of world
monetary reserves.

Let the United States, the United Kingdom, and other major
countries bar the use of their national currency as monetary reserves
by other countries. Give all countries, instead, the choice of keeping
in the form of international, gold-convertible, deposits at the International Monetary Fund, any portion of their reserves which they do
not wish to hold in the form of gold. Attach to these reserve deposits
at the Fund exchange rate guarantees that would make them a far
safer medium for reserve investment than any national currency
holdings, always exposed to devaluation, inconvertibility, blocking,
or even default by the debtor country. Let them, finally, earn interest
at a rate to be determined, and varied from time to time, in the light
of the Fund's earnings on its own loans and investments.

These various features, combining the earning incentive of foreign
exchange holdings with the safety incentive of gold holdings, should
ensure in time a large and continuing demand for Fund deposits.
In order, however, to take account of initial diffidence and inertia,
and to guarantee the system against the vagaries of sudden and unpredictable shifts between gold holdings and Fund deposits, all
countries should undertake to hold in the form of Fund deposits a
uniform and agreed proportion of their gross monetary reserves.
They would be entitled, but not compelled, to convert into gold at
the Fund any deposits accruing to their account in excess of this
minimum requirement.

A minimum deposit ratio of 20 per cent would probably be ample
to initiate the new system, and would substitute for the present,
exceedingly complex and rigid, system of national quota contri-

butions to the IMF capital. This ratio might have to be increased in time, however, in order to provide adequate lending power to the Fund, and to ensure beyond any shadow of doubt the full liquidity and convertibility of Fund deposits into gold or any currency needed for settlements. On the other hand, prudent management of the system would, in all likelihood, make it unnecessary to resort to compulsion for that purpose, as the member countries' own interest would lead them to maintain with the Fund, rather than in gold, a much larger proportion of their total reserves than the minimum percentages imposed by the Fund.

The only major objection to this proposed reform in the Fund's operations would be the same as that raised against the Keynes plan for an International Clearing Union. Such a system would endow the Fund with a lending capacity which, if improperly used, might impart a strong inflationary bias to the world economy. This danger, however, can be guarded against most effectively, simply and directly by limiting the Fund's annual lending authority to the amount necessary to preserve an adequate level of international liquidity.

Various alternative criteria could be retained for this purpose. The simplest one might be to limit the Fund's net lending, over any twelve months period, to a total amount which would, together with current increases in the world stock of monetary gold, increase total world reserves by, let us say, 3 to 5 per cent a year. The exact figure could not, of course, be determined scientifically and would, in any case, depend in practice upon the compromise between divergent national viewpoints which would emerge from the negotiation of the new Fund Agreement. A reasonably conservative solution would be to retain a 3 per cent figure as definitely non-inflationary, and to require qualified votes (two thirds, three fourths, and ultimately four fifths of the total voting power, or even unanimity) to authorize lending in excess of 3, 4 or 5 per cent a year.

The Fund's lending operations, moreover, should be no more automatic than they are at present, and this discretion should enable it to exercise a considerable influence upon members to restrain internal inflationary abuses.

A new and different category of Fund lending, however, would arise from the reform proposed here. This would consist of open-market investments in the financial markets of member countries, undertaken at the initiative of the Fund itself.

The first investments of this character would result automatically from the initial absorption by the new Fund of the outstanding national currency reserves transferred to it by members in exchange for Fund deposits. The bulk of these reserves would be in the form of bank deposits, acceptances and Treasury bills previously held by the central banks themselves in New York and London. The Fund would have no immediate need to modify the pattern of these investments, but should be empowered to do so, in a smooth and progressive manner, insofar as useful for the conduct of its own operations. This purpose would be served by giving the Fund an option—which it would not necessarily wish to use every year—of liquidating such investments at a maximum pace of, let us say, 5 per cent annually.

3. May I close now with a few words about the advantages, and disadvantages, which such a reform would entail for the United States itself.

Its major advantage emerges clearly, I hope, from our previous discussion. The United States would no longer have to bear the burden, and court the dangers, inseparable from the use of the dollar as a reserve currency by other countries. This would, it is true, deprive us of unrequited capital imports which have, in the past ten years, allowed us to carry a heavier burden of foreign lending and aid programs than we could have financed otherwise. We would now have to share these responsibilities—and the political influence that might accompany them—with other countries, through processes of multilateral decision-making which would, at times, be irritating and frustrating. We would, on the other hand, have consolidated in the hands of the Fund a large portion of highly volatile foreign funds, whose sudden and unpredictable outflow might otherwise unleash, at any time, an unbearable drain on our gold reserves. Most of all, we would have shed thereby the straitjacket which the need to prevent such an outflow would impose upon monetary management and interest rates in this country, whenever the success of our price stabilization efforts allows us to give primary consideration once more to the furtherance of maximum feasible rates of employment and economic growth.

A second, and closely related, consideration is that these reforms would put an end to an absurd situation under which we have been in practice—with only minor exceptions—the sole net lender in the IMF in spite of our persistent deficits and of the equally persistent and huge surpluses accumulated over the last ten years by other IMF members. We would, moreover, be able for the first time to obtain assistance ourselves from the IMF—through the more flexible procedure of IMF investments rather than loans—without triggering the dangerous psychological reactions which would now accompany a United States request for such assistance. The IMF itself would need to look for safe investment outlets for its expanded resources, particularly during the initial years of the new system, and this would fit in particularly well with our own need to buy the time necessary for effecting, in as smooth a manner as possible—in the interest of other countries as well as in our own—the readjustment of our current overall balance of payments deficits.

These, I think, are the essential considerations that should guide us. I should mention, however, two other points of a more technical character, but which may still be of interest to this Committee.

Our minimum deposit obligation in this new IMF can be calculated approximately, on the basis of our current position, as in the neighborhood of $4.3 billion, which is just about equal to our present Fund quota. About half of this obligation would be discharged by counting as part of our required deposit the $2.1 billion of net claims on the Fund accumulated by us as a result of past transactions. The other half, however, would have to be paid in gold, but the IMF would also cancel about $2 billion of demand deposits and Treasury certificates which it now holds against us and are now counted, I believe, as an integral part of our national debt.

It should also be noted that our deposits with the Fund should be properly regarded in a very different light from our present subscription to the Fund capital. This subscription is not now considered, and should not be considered, as a fully liquid and bankable asset. It is therefore excluded from the calculation of our monetary reserves. Our deposits with the Fund, on the other hand, would be as fully liquid as gold itself and as fully usable in all international payments. They should therefore properly be counted—in our case as in the case of other countries—as fully equivalent to gold for the calculation of monetary reserves and of legal gold cover requirements. Our monetary reserves, after the cancellation of our present quota subscription and its replacement by a 20 per cent deposit with the Fund, would actually have risen from its present level of $19.5 billion to about $21.6 billion. Most of all, our short-term liabilities to foreign countries would have declined by approximately $9 billion through the transfer to the Fund, and consolidation by it, of the liquid dollar holdings now held by these countries as monetary reserves.

These, I firmly and deeply believe, are extremely powerful arguments for a serious study of these proposals by the Administration and by Congress. I fervently hope that we shall be able to act in time, and to refute the disabused comment and dire prediction of a former colleague of mine in the Administration: "Triffin, you are very probably right, but, in this matter as in that of EPU, your proposals come several years too soon, and this time I don't honestly think you'll get anywhere until people are shaken into action by a real crisis. Then, maybe!"

This, I must admit, is probably the most widely held view on this subject at present.

Part One

Diagnosis

The Return to Convertibility: 1926–1931 and 1958–
or
Convertibility and the Morning After

> "The study of history, while it
> does not endow with prophecy,
> may indicate lines of proba-
> bility."
> JOHN STEINBECK, *The Short
> Reign of Pippin IV*

Introduction

THE 1958 CHRISTMAS WEEKEND showered upon the international
monetary world a bundle of long-awaited presents:

From Britain, the "dash to convertibility," originally envisaged
for 1953;

From France, a radical monetary reform, which promised to close
more than thirty years of uninterrupted currency inflation and
exchange rate depreciation;

From the six countries of the European Economic Community, a
first, but fateful, step on the long road toward full integration of
their national economies;

From all of these countries, and many others still, a cascade of so-
called convertibility decisions, crowning, dramatizing and consolidating previous, *de facto* progress toward the restoration of the
1920's gold exchange standard.

These momentous, and long overdue, decisions were also accompanied, however, by a dangerous breach between the six countries
of the European Economic Community and their partners in the
Organization for European Economic Cooperation, and by a decision
to liquidate the European Payments Union which had, for more
than eight years, embodied and sparked this cooperation in the
monetary field. Even the most ardent opponents of the European

17

Payments Union had long been forced to recognize the vital part played by that institution in the liquidation of early postwar bilateralism and in the progress achieved by Europe toward the restoration of a free, multilateral, system of world trade and payments. The EPU was condemned, however, by its very success in achieving its stated objective. The crutches, it was felt, could now be thrown away.[1]

This loosening of European cooperation is all the more disquieting when viewed against the background of the previous return to convertibility after World War I. The new gold standard functioned rather fitfully during the second half of the 1920's, only to be swept away in 1931 by the first gushes of the world depression. Its collapse was blamed by later writers on the incomplete nature of the 1920's so-called "restoration." The façade of the pre-1914 building had been rebuilt and repainted, but its shattered foundations and crumbling inner walls had received only the most patchwork type of repairs.[2]

This criticism held a great deal of truth, but it did not reach deep enough and pointed to the wrong conclusion. The words "restoration" and "reconstruction" suggest a mere digging up and dusting off of past institutional forms, regardless of the changes in the economic and political environment in which they have to operate. The nineteenth century monetary standard had been, on the contrary, a highly flexible and adaptable system, whose 1913 version bore little resemblance to the 1816 model. Further evolution and adaptations, rather than a mere return to the past, would have been required to fit it to the needs and conditions of the postwar world.

What was true then is even truer today. The enormous upheavals in economic philosophy, institutions and policies brought about by two world wars and the 1930's world depression have modified radically the conditions under which international convertibility can be meaningfully defined and realistically made to work today. The negative implications of this statement are only too well perceived by the 1958 planners, just as they were by their forefathers in the 1920's. The reservations and qualifications surrounding the new

1. My book on *Europe and the Money Muddle* (Yale University Press, 1957) recounts, analyzes, and appraises the 1947–1956 recovery of Europe from narrow bilateralism to *de facto* near-convertibility. Its three concluding chapters try to extract the significance of this experience for policy-makers and anticipate, on numerous points, the issues discussed in this book.

2. See particularly W. A. Brown, Jr., *The International Gold Standard Reinterpreted, 1914–1934,* New York, 1940.

convertibility decisions[3] make it abundantly clear that no country is prepared to subordinate fully and unilaterally its domestic policy aims and techniques to the maintenance of international balance, and to renounce all recourse to exchange rate adaptations and trade and exchange controls as alternative techniques of balance of payments adjustment.

What is much less clear is the positive content of this "convertibility à la 1959" and the concrete steps that may preserve it from another collapse "à la 1931," when the international economic climate changes once more from good to fair, or from fair to foul.

Two closely interrelated questions seem to me of particular urgency at this time. The first is that of preserving—or restoring—an adequate level of international reserves and liquidity in an expanding world economy, a topic which received a great deal of constructive attention at the recent meeting of the Board of Governors of the International Monetary Fund in New Delhi. It quickly leads, however, into a second and broader issue, on which complete silence was paradoxically, but tactfully, maintained at that meeting, *i.e.* the vulnerability of a world monetary system whose operation becomes increasingly dependent on one or a few *national* currencies as major components of *international* monetary reserves.[4]

The same two problems were causing widespread concern in the late 1920's and early 1930's. The Gold Delegation of the Financial Committee of the League of Nations was kept busy for nearly three years, discussing the measures needed to economize gold in short supply and to palliate the most obvious defects of the gold exchange standard.[5] Academic economists were equally stirred by these prob-

3. The new convertibility obviously will not, any more than it did in the 1920's, reintroduce internationally acceptable gold coins into the national monetary circulation of the convertible countries. It will, even more than it did then, depend very largely on foreign exchange holdings to supplement inadequate levels of gold reserves throughout the world. It will now apply to non-residents, but not necessarily to residents, to current account transactions, but not necessarily to capital movements.

4. This silence eloquently refutes any hopes that I might have otherwise entertained of having stimulated the interest of the Fund in these problems through my exhortations in *Europe and the Money Muddle*, pp. 295–301.

5. See these various publications of the League of Nations: a) *Interim Report of the Gold Delegation of the Financial Committee*, 1930. b) *Selected Documents submitted to the Gold Delegation of the Financial Committee*, 1930. c) *Second Interim Report of the Gold Delegation of the Financial Committee*, 1931. d) *Selected Documents on the Distribution of Gold Submitted to the Gold Delegation of the Financial Committee*, 1931. e) Dr. Feliks Mlynarski, *The Functioning of the Gold Standard*, 1931. f) *Report of the Gold Delegation of the Financial Committee*, 1932.

lems and, while disagreeing as always on technical details and proposed remedies, showed a rare unanimity in their criticism of the
latter system. The wisdom of these warnings was, for once, promptly
confirmed by the collapse of sterling in September 1931, the whole-
sale liquidation of the gold exchange standard, and the ensuing
aggravation of the world crisis through the spiralling of exchange
rate devaluations and of trade and exchange restrictions. In view of
this sad experience, the complacency with which we are now re-
turning to the same unorganized gold exchange standard, on an even
shakier basis than in the 1920's, is hard indeed to understand. This
may be what the Managing Director of the International Monetary
Fund, Per Jacobsson, had in mind when he reiterated in several of
his recent speeches his favorite warning from Santayana: "Those who
do not remember the past will be condemned to repeat it."

Part One of this book will focus primarily on these major threats
to the success of the new convertibility experiment. Part Two will
then try to define, on the basis of this analysis, some of the reforms
that might help adapt present-day convertibility institutions to
present-day needs and possibilities.

CHAPTER 1

Convertibility: What and How?

Convertibility Yesterday

The original meaning of the word "convertibility" has been all but forgotten in the discussions of the last ten years. It was indeed closely allied to institutional monetary and banking mechanisms totally alien to those of our days, and one of the main characteristics of which was a large and material overlapping between the national money of each country and that of its major trading partners. Except for small amounts of subsidiary coinage, the greater part of most countries' legal tender money was in the form of gold and silver coins which would either be accepted at par—or very close to par—by the residents of other countries, or be exchangeable at some Mint for any other foreign moneys needed in international settlements.[6] The convertibility problem was, to that extent, by-passed through the material equivalence of the various national currencies in terms of their gold or silver content. The gradual shift from bi-metallism to a pure gold standard progressively limited the role of silver in this respect, but was accompanied by a parallel shift from silver to gold as the major component of national monetary circulation in all the gold standard countries.[7]

The development of bank money, in the form of currency notes and demand deposits, did not at first create any specific convertibility problem. Banks were merely subject to the general obligation of discharging their own debts in legal tender money, *i.e.* initially in the gold or silver moneys of the country where they operated. If an individual bank failed to do so, bankruptcy laws would apply to it just as they would to any other individual or firm. Its own creditors

6. The ratio of gold and silver coinage to total monetary circulation, for the world at large, is estimated to have fluctuated between, roughly, 70 and 80 per cent between 1885 and 1913. See the interesting volume of Jacques E. Mertens on *La Naissance et le Développement de l'Etalon-Or*, Presses Universitaires de France, Paris, 1944, Tables 49-53.

7. See tables quoted in the preceding footnote.

would suffer thereby, but the national currency was left unaffected.

Special "convertibility" provisions had to be enacted, however, in connection with the issue of currency notes when these were granted "legal tender" status by the State. Any debtor could then discharge its obligation to its creditors by tendering such currency notes in payment, but the issuing institution itself could not claim the benefit of this provision with respect to its own i.o.u.'s. It remained obliged to redeem or "convert" them upon demand in gold (or silver) coins as defined in the country's monetary legislation.

As long as convertibility was in operation in a gold standard country, it would ensure exchange rate stability with respect to all other gold standard countries. The difficulties which might arise for the banks in connection with the maintenance of convertibility, moreover, were not necessarily related to balance of payments deficits. They might originate as well in an increased demand for internally circulating gold coins, such as might occur during a period of boom in domestic economic activity, regardless of the status of the country's balance of payments with the outside world.

A currency became "inconvertible" *de facto* or *de jure* when the issuing institution actually ceased to honor its redemption commitment, or was relieved of it by law. This did not mean, however, that currency holders would thereby be unable to convert it into gold or foreign currencies. They could usually continue to do so, but through the private market and at the rates resulting from supply and demand on that market. The original meaning of the term "inconvertibility" thus had nothing to do with true inconvertibility, in the modern sense of the world. It would be called today "exchange rate flexibility."

Convertibility Today

This radical change in the use of the term convertibility is eloquently illustrated by the proposal, so often voiced in recent official and academic discussions, to restore convertibility on the basis of flexible exchange rates, *i.e.* on the basis of what was still in the 1920's the very essence of "inconvertibility." The explanation of this paradox lies in the fact that several features of the nineteenth century international trade and payments system, more essential than exchange rate stability itself, were then taken for granted, but can no longer be taken for granted today.

The first of these was the freedom accorded to international capital movements. Most modern writers, impressed by the disequi-librating character of "hot money" movements since World War I, would regard such freedom as unessential or even undesirable today. This view was officially sanctioned by the Articles of Agreement of the International Monetary Fund which specifically authorize re-strictions on capital movements and even make them, at times, a prerequisite for a country's access to the Fund's resources.[8] The dis-cussion which follows will make clear some of my reasons for doubt-ing the practical wisdom of such an approach, and for retaining the freedom of capital movements as one of the basic characteristics of a workable system of international convertibility.

Convertibility is usually identified today with the elimination of all quantitative restrictions on trade and payments on current ac-count. This is both too much and too little, too exacting and not sufficiently exacting.

It is too little, because it leaves out of account tariff restrictions which may, if sufficiently high, unstable, or discriminatory, be even more damaging to international trade than modest, stable and non-discriminatory systems of quantitative restrictions. It is too much, because it makes no distinction between restrictions of this character and the widespread recourse to bilateral trade and payments tech-niques which may, but do not necessarily, accompany the use of trade and exchange controls.[9]

A meaningful definition of convertibility objectives must, of neces-sity, encompass all alternative techniques through which similar results may be achieved in practice. It must therefore take into ac-count trade as well as exchange techniques of restrictions, and tariff restrictions as well as quantitative restrictions. Carried to its full logical consequences, the definition of convertibility most prevalent

8. See Article VI, particularly Sections 1 and 3.

9. Such a distinction is approximated, but no more than approximated, by the line currently drawn between "resident" and "non-resident" convertibility. Convertibility of sterling for non-residents, for instance, means that sterling area residents may remain subject to various degrees of restrictions on foreign transactions, but that current earners of sterling outside the sterling area may use such earnings freely for settlements—at least on current account—not only in the sterling area, but anywhere in the world. This goes very far indeed toward the practical elimination of bilateral trade and payments techniques, but still leaves the door wide open to the application of stringent dis-criminatory restrictions on sterling area residents' trade with the countries which would otherwise use their sterling earnings in such a way as to expose the United Kingdom to a serious drain on its gold and hard currency reserves. The threat of such dis-criminatory application of restrictions on British residents could be used to exact bilateral concessions or preferences from these countries.

today—*i.e.* the elimination of all quantitative trade and exchange restrictions—should therefore lead us to confuse convertibility with the Manchesterian ideal of Free Trade.

Practical policy aims, however, can rarely be enclosed in rigid logical definitions. If we wish to designate as "convertibility" feasible goals of international economic policy, susceptible of concrete implementation in a concrete historical environment, we will have to define convertibility in relative, rather than in absolute, terms. Nineteenth century experience suggests that convertibility be defined as an institutional framework which minimizes the most harmful forms of State interference with mutually beneficial economic relations among sovereign nations. This should imply a maximum degree of multilateralism, stability and freedom in the international trade and payments system, but would not require full and unconditional compliance with any of these three criteria.

The first—multilateralism—should probably be regarded as the most crucial, and also the easiest to achieve. Its opposite extreme—bilateralism—marked the utter breakdown of convertibility in the early postwar years. The near elimination of bilateralism after 1950 was primarily the result of the European Payments Union Agreement and of the OEEC Code of Liberalization. Yet, both of these Agreements accepted implicitly some degree of discrimination as a price worth paying for the outlawing of bilateralism and the gradual lifting of quantitative restrictions in intra-European trade.

Although non-discrimination should be regarded as one of the pillars of nineteenth century convertibility, it did not operate even then as an ironclad rule in practice. Non-discrimination was then spelled out in the famous "most-favored nation" clause enshrined in most trade and tariff treaties. This clause, however, was subject to a number of qualifications and exceptions. Regional perferences—particularly within the British Empire—were traditionally allowed among some countries closely linked together by geographical, historical or political bonds. Non-discrimination was also tempered by reciprocity criteria in the case of countries—primarily the United States—which insisted on a *conditional* interpretation of the most-favored nation clause. Finally, the clause was also circumvented occasionally through ridiculously minute definitions of tariff nomenclature, designed to limit the benefits of a new concession to one or a few countries only.

Yet, these exceptions remained exceptions. Their overall quantitative impact was moderate, and they never opened the door to any significant extension of bilateralism in international trade and payments. As long as this was true, trade and tariff restrictions protected national producers against foreign competition only within their own country's boundaries. Equal access of all countries' producers to third markets preserved the full interplay of competitive forces among exporters the world over, and forced each country to maintain internationally competitive prices and costs, in order to retain a level of exports sufficient—together with other net receipts or expenditures on service and capital accounts—to finance its own payments abroad for merchandise imports.

It is indeed very tempting therefore to identitfy convertibility with multilateralism, and as perfectly compatible with a non-discriminatory, or at least non-bilateral, use of tariffs or other trade and exchange restrictions. Yet, this could lead to absurd conclusions as a criterion for international policy. Sufficiently high or unstable levels of non-discriminatory restrictions could stifle trade altogether and be far worse, as a result, than more moderate levels of moderately discriminatory restrictions. Practicable convertibility aims should make room for feasible compromises between the three ideal criteria of multilateralism, stability and freedom in the international trade and payments system.

For reasons that will soon become apparent, these compromises may have to remain short in every respect of those that could be implemented under nineteenth century conditions. Tariff restrictions were then extremely moderate by modern standards, and quantitative restrictions practically unknown. Most of all, tariff duties were changed infrequently and were often consolidated for long periods of time through trade treaty negotiations. They were used primarily for revenue or protection purposes, but hardly or not at all as a technique for balance of payments adjustments.

Since, however, no country—whether convertible or not—can escape the necessity of balancing its overall accounts with the rest of the world, the maintenance of nineteenth century convertibility depended on the implementation of other techniques of adjustment, alternative to the use of trade or exchange restrictions and of changes in exchange rates. To the extent that these nineteenth century techniques of adjustment may no longer prove workable or acceptable today, new ones will have to be put in their place, or our convertibility objectives will have to be tailored down to less ambitious criteria than those of yesterday. The exploration of these policy issues will be reserved for Part Two of this volume.

What Made Convertibility Work before World War I?

What made convertibility workable before 1914, and what made it unworkable in all of the following forty-five years, except for the brief bonfire of the late 1920's?

Theoretical and textbook discussions tend to stress primarily in their answer to these two questions the corrective mechanism of balance of payments adjustments. Classical theory emphasized the role of money flows and their impact upon "corrective" price adjustments and the restoration of a competitive pattern of international prices and costs. Modern theorists have placed greater emphasis on the mechanism of income transfers and their impact upon economic activity and employment, as well as upon prices and costs. Their analysis did not weaken, but strengthened, the classical view as to the effectiveness and equilibrating tendencies of balance of payments adjustments. It raised serious doubts, however, about the theoretical desirability and practical acceptability of such a mechanism whenever its main burden falls upon economic activity and employment rather than on price adaptations. The breakdown of convertibility after the first world war was thus ascribed to the growing rigidities which interfered with price, cost and wage adaptations, to the consequent impact of convertibility adjustments upon the levels of economic activity and employment, and to the political and social resistance which this evoked from governments and public opinion.

I have no quarrel with this analysis, but feel that it does not make sufficiently explicit some of the institutional factors which explain the success of nineteenth century convertibility.

One of these has received considerable attention from Taussig and from his students: it is the enormous scope which capital movements gave to the financing and cushioning—and therefore to the perpetuation rather than the correction—of current account disequilibria. Large, persistent and often growing disequilibria showed no sign of, or need for, correction over several decades, or even over the whole century separating the Napoleonic wars from the first world war. The net capital inflow into the United States, for instance, is estimated to have averaged $50 million a year or more throughout the period from 1850 to 1914, while the net outflow of capital from the United Kingdom rose from about $30 million a year in the first half of the century to approximately $250 million in the second half, and close to $900 million in the last years (1906–1913) before the first world war.[10]

This did not mean, of course, that all need for *corrective* adjustments was thereby eliminated, and that private capital movements would automatically cushion any trend toward imbalance in a country's international accounts. On the contrary, the availability of cushioning capital on such a scale was very much dependent on the fact that residual deficits—on current *plus* private capital account—could be expected to be corrected relatively promptly and smoothly. Yet, as long as this mechanism functioned, it made it easier for the deficit countries to accept and implement such residual adjustments without recourse to trade or exchange restrictions and, in most cases, without recourse to exchange depreciation.

The second factor which explains the successful functioning of nineteenth century convertibility lies in the fact that the emergence of *major* imbalance was *prevented ex ante* by the institutional monetary and banking framework of the times, rather than *corrected ex post* by large price and income adjustments. In spite of the greater flexibility of prices and costs in the nineteenth century, I doubt very much whether a 20 or 30 per cent reduction in wages, if called for to restore equilibrium in the balance of payments, would have been tolerated then any more than it would be today. The fact is that the ability of the system to correct such major maladjustments through internal price and income adaptations was rarely put to a test in the major Western countries which constituted the core of the system. Whenever it was put to such a test—as it repeatedly was in most Latin American countries—the correction was uniformly brought about by currency devaluation rather than by the internal adaptations postulated by the gold standard system.

Price increases and balance of payments deficits are alternative —and often complementary—forms of adaptation to an *ex ante* excess of expenditures over production. Such a gap can arise only if it is financed, and its financing, for a country as a whole, can come only from two sources: net foreign disinvestments by the non-bank

10. These estimates are derived from the *Balance of Payments Statistical Supplement* published in 1958 by the Department of Commerce (p. 10), and from Albert A. Imlah, "British Balance of Payments and Export of Capital, 1816–1913," in *Economic History Review*, 1952, pp. 208–239. See also Imlah's recent book on *Economic Elements in the Pax Britannica*, Harvard University Press, 1958.

sectors of the economy, or net borrowings from the domestic banking system.[11]

The first of these two techniques of financing leaves the banking system unaffected and does not, therefore, raise any convertibility problem as such. The inflow of funds from abroad—or the disinvestment of funds previously accumulated abroad—provides, moreover, not only the overall financing of excess expenditures, but also the foreign exchange needed to finance the excess of imports over exports. Moderate price rises would suffice to stimulate such excess imports, and these would, in turn, act as a brake on larger price increases. We have already noted above the enormous role played by such external financing in the nineteenth century balance of payments adjustments.

A peculiar form of net foreign disinvestment lay in the financing of excess expenditures from existing cash holdings of internationally acceptable gold—and initially silver—coins. As different from today, a substantial portion of the currency holdings of the public consisted in such international moneys, rather than in fiduciary claims on the domestic banking system. The financing of excess expenditure through such dishoardings of international cash would automatically provide also the foreign exchange needed to finance excess imports and limit the possible extent of domestic price rises.

Convertibility problems could only arise if the financing of excess expenditures were fed by an expansion of bank credit or a contraction of outstanding claims—particularly paper money and deposits—on the domestic monetary and banking system of the country. The difficulties to which such financing could give rise, however, were not necessarily tied to balance of payments deficits, and did not necessarily involve the fate of the national currency as such. They would focus, on the first instance, on individual banking institutions whose rate of credit expansion had been excessive in relation to others, and this could come about regardless of the balance of payments of the country as a whole. The improvident bank might be forced to suspend its payments, but this would affect only the liquidity of its

11. The Organization for European Economic Cooperation will publish in the spring of 1960 comprehensive estimates of postwar monetary developments in the seventeen member countries, in which the type of analysis briefly summarized in the above sentence is fully explained and applied to empirical data. Puzzled readers may, in the meantime, consult my discussion in *Europe and the Money Muddle*, pp. 49–53, and in "A Simplified Scheme for the Integration of Monetary and Income Analysis," in Vol. IV, pp. 293–311 of the *Memoria* of the Fifth Meeting of Technicians of Central Banks of the American Continent, published by the Banco de la República, Bogotá (Colombia), 1957.

own depositors, and not the currency of the country in general. In most cases, of course, Central Bank assistance would be made available in time to meet the problem, but again not on a scale endangering the liquidity of the Central Bank itself and the solidity of the national currency. The other credit operations of the Central Bank, both with its private customers and with the State, would also be geared to the preservation of its own liquidity position, rather than to national objectives such as the maintenance of full employment, price stability or balance of payments equilibrium.

These financial traditions created, wherever they were observed, the most effective barrier against inflationary excesses susceptible of entailing large-scale price and cost maladjustments. They were, of course, dependent themselves on the predominantly *laissez faire* philosophy of the influential financial, economic and political circles of each country. Occasional departures from these accepted canons of behavior might be forced upon the authorities by foreign or civil war, but were mostly limited to underdeveloped countries not linked politically to the West. Outside of such accidents, the major fluctuations in prices and economic activity were roughly parallel among the major trading countries and required only moderate, and thus feasible, readjustments to preserve currency convertibility.

The Collapse of Convertibility after World War I

This spontaneous harmonization of internal financial policies has been hopelessly shattered as a result of the two world wars and, even more, of the world depression. New philosophies and techniques of national policies have emerged which subordinate, whenever the two enter into conflict, the preservation of exchange freedom and stability to other and overriding national objectives. These new techniques involve, in the field of trade and finance:

1. the extensive use of the issue power of central banks to underwrite the State's own deficits and, in addition, the credit expansion of other banks whenever such expansion conforms to the wishes, or even merely to the existing regulations, of the national monetary authorities;

2. the unwillingness to subordinate fully such credit policies to the preservation or restoration of a competitive price and cost pattern and of an overall external balance, at current prices and exchange rates, compatible with the amount of gold and foreign exchange resources available, or accessible, to the monetary authorities;

3. the recourse to currency depreciation, to trade and exchange restrictions, or even to generalized rationing controls, or a combination of such measures, whenever the country is forced by the exhaustion, or near exhaustion, of its monetary reserves to adjust its external expenditures to its external receipts.

The broad consequences of this institutional evolution for the world's trade and payments system have been the breakdown of the gold standard during the interwar and postwar periods, *i.e.* the generalization of exchange rate instability and of trade and exchange restrictions. The breakdown was a gradual one and culminated in the unbridled bilateralism of the early postwar years. The disadvantages of such a system, for each country as well as for the international community as such, finally became sufficiently obvious to all to prompt patient and determined efforts to reverse the process and restore freedom and stability in external trade and payments arrangements.

I shall reserve for later discussion the examination of the techniques which have proved most feasible and successful in this respect, and concentrate attention at this stage on the impact of the policies described above on capital movements and the role of monetary reserves.

CHAPTER 2

The Changing Role
of Monetary Reserves

These radical changes in the international and national monetary and banking systems have fundamentally altered the role of monetary reserves and other capital movements in balance of payments adjustments.

Current discussions of reserve requirements stress primarily the role of reserves in the cushioning of balance of payments deficits, and rely for an approximate, and admittedly very rough, measurement of reserve adequacy on the ratio of a country's overall reserves to annual imports or exchange sales. Such a concept would have been largely alien to nineteenth century writers, and did not indeed play any prominent role in either academic or policy analyses of the problem until the second world war.[1] Legal prescriptions on monetary reserves and monetary issues varied widely from country to country, but never made any reference to a country's export or import levels. They were concerned exclusively and directly with the avoidance of excessive currency issues and relied for this purpose either on an overall ceiling on such issues, or on the limitation of fiduciary issues— *i.e.* the amounts that could be issued over and above the metallic reserves held as counterpart by the issuing bank—or on a minimum ratio of reserves to note issues or sight liabilities. This latter criterion was the one that conformed most closely to practical bankers' experience as to their own liquidity requirements, and tended more and more to determine legal or customary standards of reserve adequacy. The maintenance of a ratio of about one third between liquid reserves and sight obligations gradually became the usual minimum

1. Its explicit recognition as one of several criteria for Central Bank management was introduced for the first time in Central Bank legislation in 1944. See the author's *Monetary and Banking Reform in Paraguay*, Board of the Governors of the Federal Reserve System, Washington, 1946, pp. 82–84, and 136–37.

benchmark for central bank as well as for commercial bank operations.

It hardly need be said that this could result in extremely disparate ratios between central bank reserves and the level of the country's imports. This ratio can be estimated, for instance, to have been less than 5 per cent for the Bank of England in 1913, as compared to more than 40 per cent for the Bank of France.[2] This contrast was not without significance for monetary management, and complaints were often voiced against the frequency with which the Bank of England had to resort to changes in the discount rate in order to protect its slender level of reserves. The Bank, however, was a private firm, motivated by the search for profits as well as by broader considerations of public service, and showed great reluctance to accumulate non-earning gold assets greatly in excess of liquidity requirements as judged in the light of its own experience in the past. Private capital movements were regarded as the normal source of cushioning for balance of payments fluctuations, and could be hastened, whenever necessary, by open market operations and changes in the discount rate. The main test of this mechanism, from the Bank's point of view, lay in the fact that any substantial drain on its gold reserves could be arrested long before it would endanger the Bank's own liquidity.

The radical changes imparted to monetary institutions and policies by the first world war and the world depression have completely revolutionized the role of monetary reserves and have consequently brought about fundamentally different views as to their measurement and adequacy.

First of all, the universal disappearance of gold coin from active monetary circulation has deeply modified the significance of central bank liquidity. Reserves need no longer be held to convert bank deposits and paper currency into legal gold tender for purposes of domestic circulation. Reserve drains are now associated exclusively with external deficits in the balance of payments of the country. In a closed economy, central bank liquidity would be fully assured by its mere ability to print notes. Excessive issues would be reflected

2. Only a minor portion of this striking contrast is due to the difference in the ratio of gold reserves to liabilities for the two banks (approximately 35% for the Bank of England, and 50% for the Bank of France). Most of it can be ascribed to the much greater role played in England by private bank deposits in total money supply and by the much higher ratio of imports, and lower ratio of money, to GNP in England as compared to France.

in inflationary pressures upon prices, but would not affect the bank's liquidity.

Secondly, international flows of private capital can no longer be relied upon as a major source of cushioning for current account disequilibria. Fears of currency depreciation and exchange restrictions often indeed tend to stimulate private capital flows from deficit countries to surplus countries, and to aggravate, rather than cushion, the impact of current account imbalance.[3] These movements of "hot money" played a particularly large role in the interwar period and continue even today to elude, in many cases, the nets of exchange control legislation. On the other hand, the unprecedented development of official loans and grants provides today vast amounts of cushioning capital, which substitute in part for the private capital flows of the gold standard era. The International Monetary Fund, the International Bank for Reconstruction and Development, the European Payments Union, the European Fund, the European Investment Bank, the Colombo Plan, etc. were specifically set up for that purpose. France and England have also stepped up enormously financial aid to their overseas territories and associated monetary areas. The Marshall Plan and other U.S. foreign aid programs completely dwarfed, in the early postwar years, the rather modest flows of private investments abroad and still account today—even excluding military grants—for about half of the United States total capital exports.

Official grants and loans, however, cannot be regarded as a normal and dependable source of financing for short-run disequilibria. They usually require long and uncertain negotiations whose ultimate success may also be made dependent at times on political or economic conditions unacceptable to the prospective borrower. In spite of the more flexible and automatic procedures recently developed by the International Monetary Fund—and, up to its recent demise, by the European Payments Union—countries must still look today to their own monetary reserves as their first and most important line of defense against temporary deficits in their balance of payments.

The main function of monetary reserves is no longer to preserve the overall liquidity of individual central banks, but to permit the

3. International political tensions are a further factor of instability which would continue to paralyze or distort capital flows even if full confidence could be restored in the wisdom of economic policies proper.

financing of short-run deficits in the country's external transactions. The types of deficits which may appropriately be met in this manner fall into two categories. The first is that of reversible deficits reflecting purely temporary fluctuations in foreign receipts and expenditures on current and capital account. Such deficits should obviously be financed, rather than prevented or immediately corrected by policy action. Basic policy adjustments—such as deflation or devaluation—to temporary factors of imbalance would indeed sow the seeds of more fundamental and lasting imbalance in the country's economy. The shortage of reserves is more likely to induce, in such cases, a recourse to trade or exchange restrictions which would have been perfectly avoidable otherwise.

The second case is that of more fundamental disequilibria, calling for corrective action, but in which the most appropriate and desirable remedies will act relatively slowly and smoothly, and leave residual needs for the financing of tapering off deficits.

In both cases, an insufficient level of reserves will force the deficit country to resort to otherwise unnecessary measures of deflation, devaluation or restrictions to keep its payments in closer and more continuous balance with its receipts than would be called for by the need to preserve long-run equilibrium in its international transactions.

CHAPTER 3

Reserve Measurement and Adequacy Criteria

These deep-seated changes in the role of monetary reserves entail corresponding changes in their methods of measurement and criteria for adequacy. Neither, however, can be couched in any precise and clear-cut formula, invariant from time to time and from country to country. Reserves have to be higher in an unstable economic and political environment than in a world enjoying a greater degree of economic and political stability. Higher reserves are also needed by underdeveloped countries, with more volatile levels of export proceeds and capital imports, than by the richer and more diversified economies of the industrial countries. The burden of reserve accumulation, however, in relation to national wealth and savings on the one hand, and to competing needs for the financing of developmental imports on the other, will unfortunately be higher for the former countries than for the latter. In this balancing of needs and costs, the underdeveloped countries are likely therefore to assign a lower priority than the more developed countries to a reserve level adequate to eschew or minimize undesirable resort to devaluation or restrictions.

The appraisal of reserve needs for any individual country, at any particular time, would have to take these and other factors into account. The order of magnitude of future deficits calling for reserve financing might first be gauged quantitatively on the basis of past experience. This first approximation should then be revised, upward or downward, in the light of other pertinent evidence about the probable course of external and internal developments.[1]

1. The ratio of reserves to money and other liquid claims on the banking system may be of particular relevance, for instance, if past "compensatory" policies have pushed the ratio of such liquid claims to GNP to an abnormally high level. The current status of private banks' cash reserves and the strength or weakness of the legal or regulatory controls exercised by the monetary authorities over the banks' credit policy will also influence the speed with which corrective action may be applied in case of need.

Such a line of approach, however, cannot be used in a broad survey of world liquidity requirements, such as the one which will now engage our attention. Availability of data and simplicity of calculation inevitably dominate the choice of measurement methods applicable to such comprehensive inter-temporal and inter-country comparisons. Their results would admittedly be too crude to determine any precise level of reserve adequacy, but they will prove more than sufficient to indicate whether current and prospective reserve levels are likely to facilitate, or seriously hamper, the smooth functioning of international currency convertibility.

The ratio of gross reserves to annual imports will be retained in all that follows as a first, and admittedly rough, approach to the appraisal of reserve adequacy. The main reason for this choice, I must confess, is the fact that the recent study of the IMF staff on *World Reserves and Liquidity*[2] conveniently presents such ready-made calculations for eleven prewar and postwar years for all regions of the world and for more than sixty individual countries. The second is that this ratio is the one that has been most popularized in all postwar discussions of the subject, and that monetary authorities in many countries are apt to think today of reserve adequacy in these terms, and to act accordingly.[3]

It should finally be noted that the estimates of monetary reserves used in these calculations give an exaggerated impression on definiteness and of comparability over time and over space. Methods of reporting are not uniform in all countries, and, most of all, the true "reserve" character of the sterling assets reported varied considerably over the period. The usability and acceptability of "transferable," and particularly "bilateral," sterling accounts were severely limited in the early postwar years. This was of minor importance to countries

2. Washington, 1958.

3. My own preference would have gone otherwise to a ratio of reserves to balance of payments *receipts*—rather than expenditures—on current—rather than merely merchandise—account, but including also net private unilateral transfers which play an important equilibrating role in several countries' balances of payments. The arguments that may be marshalled for and against this view are not worth retaining the attention of the reader, since the matter is only of academic interest, both methods of measurement leading to similar results in all but very few cases.

Economic students should devote some time, instead, to the closely reasoned and suggestive discussion of reserve adequacy by Tibor Scitovsky in *Economic Theory and Western European Integration*. Stanford University Press, 1958, pp. 101–109. The ratio of monetary reserves to money supply, or to a broader concept of relatively liquid liabilities, also deserves more attention than it receives in the IMF study referred to in the preceding footnote.

normally in deficit with the United Kingdom or the sterling area, but highly significant for countries whose bilateral deficits with other countries—particularly in the dollar area—could not be settled through the use of such sterling balances.

Moreover, the Fund's attempted breakdown of foreign exchange reserves into their major components (sterling, dollar, EPU and BIS claims) can only be regarded as a rough approximation. This qualification, once again, applies particularly to *official* holdings of sterling, for which estimates have only recently been made available and only for the end of 1945, 1951 and 1957 (in *Economic Trends,* May 1958, p. viii). The Fund's estimates incorrectly include as official reserves all sterling holdings except those held in the United Kingdom's colonies and in the dollar area.

Important as they would be for a more refined analysis, these qualifications are not too damaging for the broad appraisal of reserve adequacy to which we shall now turn. They will be duly noted again in the few cases in which our conclusions, based on rough orders of magnitude only, could be significantly affected by them.

CHAPTER 4

Reserve Adequacy at the End
of 1957

Reserve levels, as of the end of 1957, may be appraised first in the light of past experience and, secondly, with reference to what may be known, or guessed at, of individual countries' own estimates of their reserve requirements.

The Overall Historical Record: 1913–1957

Gold and foreign exchange reserves for the world as a whole were estimated by the Fund at about 49 per cent of imports at the end of 1957, compared with 42 per cent in 1928 and only 21 per cent in 1913; and gold reserves alone to 35 per cent, compared to 32 per cent in 1928 and only 19 per cent in 1913.[1] These estimates, however, exclude gold coin in circulation outside Central Banks and Treasuries. This exclusion is hardly defensible in view of the large role which private gold holdings played before the first world war in balance of payments adjustments. While not directly under the control of the monetary authorities, they often constituted a powerful adjunct to central bank reserves in times of difficulties.[2] If gold circulation is taken into account, the ratio of monetary gold to imports shows up in 1957 as about equal to that of either 1913 or 1928 (35 to 36 per cent). This, however, was rather low by previous standards,[3]

1. *International Reserves and Liquidity*, p. 18.

2. In his study on *British International Gold Movements and Banking Policy, 1881-1913* (Harvard University Press, 1935), W. Edwards Beach draws attention to the high inverse correlation between foreign and internal movements of gold, both in the United States (p. 146) and in the United Kingdom (pp. 76–77). External gold drains in settlement of balance of payments deficits were partly fed and offset by the simultaneous contraction in the internal circulation of gold coin and its reflux toward the Bank.

3. Spot calculations for the late nineteenth century, based on estimates of the Gold Delegation of the League of Nations, yielded a ratio of about 38 per cent in 1873, 1880 and 1890, but of approximately 45 per cent in 1868 and 1897.

far lower than in the 1930's (about 100 per cent) and substantially lower than in the late 1940's (55 to 60 per cent).

Such comparisons are not very relevant, and this for a variety of reasons.

First of all, foreign exchange reserves have played since the first world war a much larger role in the world monetary system than they did in the nineteenth century. These reserves consist very largely in the short-term foreign liabilities of the United States and the United Kingdom whose *gross* reserve position in relation to imports can no longer, therefore, be regarded as an appropriate measure of these countries' liquidity. Any average ratio of gross reserves to imports for the world as a whole is highly misleading for that reason alone, and, moreover, totally unrepresentative, because of the excessive weight given to the abnormally high reserves of the United States and the admittedly low reserves of the United Kingdom.

The least objectionable procedure is to consider separately the position of these two countries as world monetary centers, and to confine attention at this stage to the gold and foreign exchange position of countries other than the United States and the United Kingdom.

The ratio of these other countries' total reserves to their imports is just about equal to what it was in 1913, but substantially lower than in any of the other years recorded in Table 3.

We may discard immediately as far in excess of minimum requirements the abnormally high ratios of reserves to imports which prevailed in the 1930's. These were indeed the combined result of widespread devaluations and of catastrophic declines in the value of world trade.

We should also discount somewhat the high reserve levels shown for the early years following World War II, since these were swollen by large holdings of inconvertible sterling, which could hardly be regarded as fully equivalent to international reserves. Nobody indeed would suggest that the international reserves position was more comfortable and adequate in the early postwar years than it is today.

The radical institutional changes which have taken place since 1913 and 1928 also preclude any direct comparisons with those years. The fact that current reserves are *lower* than they were then, however, may be retained as significant, since these changes are all of such a nature as would require a *higher* ratio of reserves to imports to facilitate the maintenance of convertibility in the face of a greater

40 PART ONE: DIAGNOSIS

variability in national policies and of far less favorable conditions
as to the size and direction of capital movements in times of crisis.
It should not be forgotten, moreover, that serious worries about the
adequacy of reserves existed also in 1928 and had prompted at the
time an extensive investigation by the Financial Committee of the
League of Nations.[4]

TABLE 3
Ratio of Monetary Reserves to Annual Imports, 1913-1957
(in per cent)

| | All Countries | | | All Countries, excluding the US and the UK | | | | | |
| | | | | | | Foreign Exchange | | | |
	Total	Gold	Foreign Exchange	Total	Gold	Total	Dollar	Sterling	EPU-BIS
Including Gold in Circulation:									
1913	39	36	2	35	32	3			
1928	46	35	11	44	28	16			
Excluding Gold in Circulation:									
1913	22	19	2	20	17	3			
1928	43	32	11	42	26	16			
1932	97	89	8	85	74	11			
1937	100	92	8	55	44	12			
1938	118	110	8	62	51	11	3	8	—
1947	87	61	26	54	19	35	5	31	—
1948	78	55	23	46	15	31	6	25	—
1949	73	55	18	40	16	24	6	17	—
1950	80	57	23	49	19	30	10	18	1
1951	58	42	16	37	15	22	7	13	1
1952	59	42	17	38	16	22	8	11	2
1953	64	45	19	44	18	26	11	12	3
1954	64	44	20	44	18	26	12	12	3
1955	58	40	18	42	18	24	12	10	2
1956	54	37	17	39	17	22	11	8	2
1957	50	35	15	35	16	19	9	7	2

Sources and Notes: see Table 14, pp. 72-73.

Only one fact need be retained from the record examined up to
now. Reserves at the end of 1957 were at an all time low in relation
to the last hundred years, and had been declining at a rather alarming pace since the end of 1954. They represented 35 per cent of
annual imports for all countries other than the United States and the
United Kingdom, taken as a group. Can anything more be said about

4. See above, p. 19 and footnote 5.

the probable adequacy or inadequacy of such a level of reserves for
the maintenance of a workable system of international convertibility?

National Reserve Requirements under Convertibility

For reasons amply discussed in previous chapters of this study,[5] the
appraisal of desirable and feasible reserve levels in relation to imports varies enormously from country to country. In addition to the
structural factors mentioned in this discussion and which facilitate
or hamper the maintenance of high reserve levels (relative levels of
wealth and savings, ratios of bank money to total money, and of
money and imports to GNP, etc.), some countries are less able or in-
sistent than others in restraining inflationary pressures and in avoid-
ing recourse to trade and exchange restrictions.

The Fund's study lays great stress on these variations. A series
of tables stresses the enormous differences in reserve ratios from
country to country as well as from one year to another. In 1957,
reserves were only 1 per cent of imports in Bolivia, but 137 per cent
in Portugal. The number of industrial countries—excluding the
United States and the United Kingdom—with reserves below 30 per
cent of imports doubled—from one fourth to one half of their total
number—between 1955 and 1957. In the latter year, twenty-seven
per cent of the non-industrial countries showed reserve ratios inferior
to 20 per cent, as against eight per cent only four years earlier.

These wide variations conceal, however, some broad trends and
regularities duly noted in the Fund's report. Thus, a large number
of non-industrialized countries unwillingly accumulated abnormally
high reserves in wartime, but drew heavily on them for re-stocking
and development when supplies became again available. The average reserve ratio for this group of countries thus fell from 73 per
cent in 1948 to 37 per cent in 1957. Continental Western Europe, on
the other hand, suffered heavy reserve losses in wartime and in the
early postwar years, but more than doubled its reserves between
1948 and 1957.

Within each group, some countries—such as Switzerland, Portugal,
Venezuela, Iraq, and Iran—persistently tend, for a variety of reasons,
to maintain relatively high reserve levels, while others—Norway,
Denmark, Yugoslavia, Israel, Malaya, Canada and South Africa, for

5. See particularly pp. 32 and 35.

instance—seem to be satisfied with reserve levels well below 30 or even 20 per cent of imports.[6]

The differences in national conditions and policies reflected in these estimates are not as significant as would seem at first—and as the Fund's study sometimes suggests[7]—for an appraisal of liquidity

TABLE 4
Variations in Regional Reserve Levels

	1928	1937	1948	1957
I. *In per cent of Imports*	43	109	89	55
A. Continental OEEC	46	78	40	42
B. Non-Industrial Areas	42	51	73	37
1. Latin America	47	51	44	41
2. Outer Sterling Countries . . .	28	46	95	41
3. Other Countries (1)	50	67	74	30
C. Canada	7	21	33	29
D. United Kingdom	13	81	24	21
E. United States	85	358	303	161
II. *In per cent of World's Gross Reserves*	100	100	100	100
A. Continental OEEC	39	24	13	28
B. Non-Industrial Areas	25	14	28	21
1. Latin America	9	3	6	7
2. Outer Sterling Countries . . .	6	5	16	8
3. Other Countries (1)	11	6	7	6
C. Canada	1	1	2	3
D. United Kingdom	6	15	4	4
E. United States	29	46	25	43

Footnote: 1. Including Japan.
Source: International Reserves and Liquidity, Appendix Table 1, pp. 100-101. Discrepancies between these estimates and the global estimates of Table 3 are due to minor discrepancies in the Fund's estimates themselves, but primarily to the exclusion of colonial territories from the present table.

requirements for the world as a whole, under conditions of monetary convertibility. There are two reasons for this. The first is that few of the countries with persistently low reserves account for a significant proportion of total world trade, while most of the large trading countries traditionally hold reserves well in excess of 30 per cent. The second is that most of the countries with low reserves also maintain much more stringent trade and exchange restrictions than the

6. See *International Reserves and Liquidity*, pp. 46–55, and Table 4 in the text. Substantial reserve declines in the non-industrialized areas, however, occurred between the end of the war and 1948 and are not shown in the table.

7. See, for instance, the comments on p. 73 of the Fund's study.

4. RESERVE ADEQUACY, 1957

TABLE 5

Average Reserve Levels, 1953-1955

(All countries, excluding the United States and the United Kingdom)

National Ratio of Reserves to Imports	Average Ratio of Reserves to Imports	Number of Countries	Proportion of Total Imports	Proportion of Total Reserves
I. *Reserves Below 33% of Imports:* Yugoslavia (6), Denmark (13), Norway (15), Paraguay (16), Bolivia and Chile (18), Peru and Spain (19), Haiti and Israel (21), Costa-Rica (22), Nicaragua and Iceland (23), Taiwan and South Africa (25), Malaya (26), Sweden (27), Syria and Finland (29), Colombia (31).	22%	21	20%	9%
II. *Reserves from 33% to 50% of Imports:* Dominican Republic and France (33), Mexico, Korea and New Zealand (34), Philippines (35), Honduras and Ecuador (36), Brazil (37), Indonesia (38), Canada (39), Lebanon (40), Turkey and Belgium (42), Italy (43), Japan and the Netherlands (45), Ireland (46), Vietnam (47), Venezuela (49), Guatamala and Salvador (50).	40%	22	52%	43%
III. *Reserves above 50% of Imports:* Argentina (51), Ceylon and Austria (52), Germany (54), Panama (56), Greece (60), Australia (61), Burma (76), Cuba (78), Ethiopia (81), Iran (85), Thailand (89), Pakistan (101), Iraq (106), Uruguay (110), India (136), Egypt and Switzerland (137), Portugal (180).	81%	19	28%	48%
Total	48%	62	100%	100%

Source: International Reserves and Liquidity, Appendix Table 1, pp. 100-101.

others. Both of these facts are brought out in Tables 5 and 6. What they suggest is that:

1. Some countries may indeed continue to hold relatively low reserves, but are also likely to have great difficulties in restoring and

maintaining convertibility, unless assured of other sources of finance in times of need.[8]

2. The maintenance of international convertibility, however, depends primarily on the policies of the major trading countries, and the avoidance of trade and exchange restrictions by them is clearly related to their ability to maintain adequate reserve levels.[9]

TABLE 6

Evolution of Twelve Major Trading Countries' Reserves, 1950-1957

(percentage ratio of reserves to imports)

	1950	1951	1952	1953	1954	1955	1956	1957	Number of cases		
									below 20%	*20-32%*	*33% and above*
Canada . .	55	44	42	38	43	37	31	29	—	2	6
Germany . .	10	15	31	52	58	53	65	75	2	1	5
France . .	44	20	23	24	32	44	24	13	1	5	2
Netherlands .	29	24	47	52	45	40	29	26	—	4	4
Belgium . .	38	40	42	44	41	40	35	33	—	—	8
Italy . . .	59	46	39	39	43	46	41	42	—	—	8
Japan . . .	58	46	54	37	43	54	47	24	—	1	7
Australia . .	92	47	52	93	61	39	49	68	—	—	8
Brazil . . .	61	26	26	46	30	38	50	32	—	4	4
Switzerland .	150	120	138	150	141	124	107	98	—	—	8
India . . .	172	105	102	146	137	127	80	43	—	—	8
Venezuela .	56	49	51	52	46	48	75	77	—	—	8
Total . .									3	17	76

Source: International Reserves and Liquidity, Appendix Table 1, pp. 100-101.

3. The reserve requirements of the latter countries exercise an overwhelming influence—as compared to those of the smaller trading countries—on the world demand for monetary reserves.

Table 5 classifies the sixty-two countries (other than the United States and the United Kingdom) for which reserves are reported by the Fund into three groups, on the basis of their average ratio of

8. The proposals developed in Part Two, Chapter 4 below (pp. 102–120) would greatly expand the capacity of the International Monetary Fund to provide such assistance.

9. Bilateralism will remain confined to a very minor portion of world trade at most as long as the United States, Canada and Western Europe—with which most of the other countries' trade also takes place—refuse to participate in bilateral agreements. The functioning of the nineteenth century gold standard depended essentially on the policies of the major trading countries, and was never endangered by the exchange rate instability of other countries, particularly in Latin America. The same would hold today for exchange restrictions outside Europe and North America.

reserves to imports over the three most "normal" years of the postwar period, *i.e.* 1953–1955. The number of countries in each group is approximately the same, but those with reserves lower than 33 per cent of imports accounted for only one fifth of total imports, and for less than one tenth of total reserves. All of them, moreover, were characterized by much tighter trade and exchange restrictions than those applied by most of the countries with higher reserve levels.

The other forty-one countries accounted for 80 per cent of the total imports, and more than 90 per cent of the total monetary reserves, of the sixty-two countries taken together. They included all the European countries outside of Scandinavia and Iceland, and all the other countries with imports in excess of $1 billion a year, except South Africa and Malaya. It is these countries' policies—and, of course, those of the United States and the United Kingdom—that will overwhelmingly determine the fate of the present convertibility experiment. These policies will be very largely influenced, in turn, by these countries' ability to preserve reserve levels sufficient to eschew unnecessary resort to trade and exchange restrictions. And it is the global level of these reserve requirements in relation to available supplies from gold production and other sources—primarily dollar and sterling balances—that will play a crucial role in determining the adequacy or inadequacy of world reserve levels for the maintenance of convertibility tomorrow.

Twelve of these forty-one countries accounted for about 60 per cent of the total imports of the sixty-two countries taken together, and for 65 per cent of their total monetary reserves. Their actual reserve ratios in each of the eight years 1950–1957 are shown in Table 6. Only in three cases did they fall below 20 per cent. Two of these refer to Germany in 1950 and 1951, before that country had emerged from the economic and financial prostration in which the war had left it. The third is that of France in the middle of a severe exchange crisis in 1957. In seventeen other cases, reserves were below 33 per cent of imports. Nine of those occurred in France and Brazil and were accompanied by severe exchange controls. In all seventy-six of the other cases observed, reserves were maintained throughout above 33 per cent of imports.

The overall record of these eight postwar years strongly suggests that most of the major countries would aim at maintaining a reserve level of not less than 40 per cent in most years, feel impelled to adopt severe readjustment measures if this level fell below, let us say, 30 or 33 per cent, and consider themselves forced to adopt drastic measures of control in the face of any persistent or substantial contraction below that critical range.[10] A 20 per cent level of gross reserves would be widely regarded as an absolute minimum, to be earmarked for rare emergencies such as the outbreak of war, or as necessary collateral for the negotiation of short or medium term loans abroad.

Under normal conditions, the actual amount of reserves in excess of 33 per cent held by some countries would far outweigh the deficiencies of other countries' reserves in relation to this level. There can be little doubt, therefore, that the 35 per cent *average* level reached in 1957 by all countries outside the United States and the United Kingdom was on the low side of any reasonable estimate of world liquidity requirements, and that any further contraction below that level would make it very difficult for a number of key countries to adhere firmly to the convertibility policies which they would otherwise be willing and eager to pursue.

If this conclusion is accepted, two further questions must be asked:

1. Is the prospective development and supply of reserves over the next few years likely to alleviate or intensify the present reserve shortage for countries other than the United States and the United Kingdom?

2. How should we appraise the present and prospective reserve position of the two center countries of the present gold exchange standard system, *i.e.* the United States and the United Kingdom?

The next two chapters will try to shed some light on these problems.

10. The Fund's study (p. 48) also remarks that most industrialized countries "appear to have tried to achieve reserve ratios of between 30 and 50 per cent, or perhaps 40 and 50 per cent, in the sense that if reserves were below these levels they tried to increase reserves, and if reserves rose beyond some such level, they saw fit to adopt a more expansionary policy."

CHAPTER 5

Prospective Adequacy of Reserves over the Ten Years 1958–1967

Prospective Reserve Needs

The Fund's study on *International Reserves and Liquidity* calculates the growth of reserves which would appear necessary over the next ten years to prevent a further decline of world reserves in relation to world imports.

The Fund bases these calculations on the assumption of an average growth rate of 3 per cent a year. For the ten years 1957–66, world reserves would have to increase by $19 billion, as against roughly $7 billion expected from the monetization of new gold production and sales of USSR gold over this period. The Fund then proceeds to lower the required $19 billion to $8 billion by considering as unlikely any increase in the reserves of four high reserve countries, *i.e.* the United States, Germany, Switzerland and Venezuela. The minor gap thus left between the required growth of reserves and the amounts expected from new gold production and USSR sales should not cause any serious worry, as it may easily be bridged, and indeed more than bridged, by a further growth of foreign exchange reserves—primarily dollar balances—and by a possible decline in private gold and dollar holdings.[1]

These optimistic conclusions are open to serious questions. First and foremost is the 3 per cent growth rate assumed as "normal" by the Fund. The data which underlie this assumption are presented on page 70 of the Fund's study, and are condensed here in Table 7. They would hardly suggest a growth rate as low as 3 per cent. The general picture that emerges is rather one of an expanding growth

---

1. See *International Reserves and Liquidity*, pp. 69–75.

rate of roughly 3 to 4 per cent in the rather depressed period of the 1880's and 1890's, of 4 per cent or more in the last decade preceding the first world war, and of 6 to 7 per cent a year both in the 1920's and in the post World War II period. The 3 per cent rate assumed by the Fund becomes plausible only when "normal" peacetime ex-

TABLE 7

Average Annual Rates of Growth of Trade and Manufacturing, 1876-1957
(*in per cent; compound basis*)

	Trade		Manu-facturing Activity
	Primary Products	Manu-factured Products	
I. *During War Years and the 1930's Depression*			
A. From 1913 to 1920			−1
B. From 1913 to 1921-25	−1.5	−2.6	0.3
C. From 1926-29 to 1931-35 . . .	−1.9	−5.7	−1.5
D. From 1938 to 1948	0		3.7
II. *During "Normal" Peace-Time Years*			
A. From 1876-80 to 1901-05 . . .	3.3	2.8	4.1
B. From 1901-05 to 1913	3.5	4.7	4.2
C. From 1921-25 to 1926-29 . . .	6.3	7.1	6.8
D. From 1948 to 1956	7.5		6.1
E. From 1950 to 1956	6.5		5.7
F. From 1950 to 1957	6.3		5.1
G. From 1951 to 1957	5.4		5.0

Sources: Estimates for "normal" years are from the IMF study on *International Reserves and Liquidity*, Table 17, p. 70.

Estimates for war years and the 1930's depression have been calculated from the indices given in the original source (LEAGUE OF NATIONS, *Industrialization and Foreign Trade*, 1945, pp. 130 and 157) and quoted on p. 104 of the IMF study. Average rates of growth for these years are not shown separately in this study (except for 1938-1948) but merged into average rates over longer periods.

perience is diluted with the abnormally low, and in fact predominantly *negative,* growth rates of wartime years and of the 1930's world depression. An expected adequacy of reserves based upon the assumption of a third world war or of another deep and protracted world depression is hardly encouraging as a guide to policy. The least that should be done, it seems to me, would be to present alternative calculations based on different rates of growth, ranging from, let us say, 3 to 6 per cent a year. This has been done in Table 8 below.[2]

A second source of underestimation in the Fund's calculations is the exclusion of high reserve countries—the United States, Switzerland, Germany and Venezuela—without any parallel upward ad-

TABLE 8

Increases in World Reserves Corresponding to Various Rates of Growth

(in billions of U.S. dollars)

| | at growth rate of | | | |
	3%	4%	5%	6%
I. *Over the Ten Years 1958-1967*				
1. All Countries	18.5	25.8	33.7	42.3
2. Excluding United States, Germany, Switzerland and Venezuela	7.5	10.4	13.7	17.2
3. Including reconstitution of 40% reserve level by the U.K. and France	12.7	16.2	20.0	24.1
4. Per cent of (3) covered by assumed supplies from new gold production and USSR sales	55%	43%	35%	29%
II. *In 1967*, on basis of assumption (3) above				
1. In billions of U.S. dollars	1.0	1.5	2.0	2.6
2. Per cent covered by assumed supplies from new gold production and USSR sales . .	70%	48%	35%	27%

Sources: 1. Reserve estimates as of the end of 1957 are taken from the January 1959 issue of *International Financial Statistics* ($53,600 for all countries, $31,864 million for the United States, Germany, Switzerland and Venezuela taken together, and $3,149 million for the United Kingdom and France, leaving an initial shortfall of $3,883 millions of reserves for these two countries with relation to 40% of their 1957 import levels as estimated in the same publication).

2. The estimated increase in the world's monetary gold over the ten years 1958-1967 ($7 billion) is taken from the IMF study on *International Reserves and Liquidity*, p. 72.

justment for any of the low reserve countries. On the contrary, the Fund's study comments (p. 72) that "it may be doubted whether all other countries would in fact wish to increase their reserves so much." This statement is formally correct, but also highly misleading.

2. It might also be noted that all these calculations with reference to an assumed rate of *physical* growth leave aside the impact of price rises upon liquidity requirements. This is, of course, reasonable insofar as one should not plan to increase international liquidity in such a way as to facilitate or stimulate inflationary price increases. Yet, if such increases are not avoided in fact by the major trading countries, corresponding liquidity adaptations might be preferable to alternative adjustments such as gold revaluation or, certainly, a tightening of trade or exchange restrictions.

While it is probably true that not *all* of these countries will increase their absolute amount of reserves sufficiently to avoid a further decline in their already low reserve ratios, one would expect such declines to be far more than offset by the reconstitution of adequate reserve levels by *some* at least of the countries which emphatically and rightly proclaim such an increase essential to enable them to achieve and consolidate a satisfactory rate of progress toward full currency convertibility.

Table 8 adjusts the Fund's estimates for such an increase in the reserve levels of two countries only: France and the United Kingdom. The postulated increase in the reserves of these countries is one that would bring them to 40 per cent of imports. This would correspond, as of the end of 1957, to a $4,564 million reserve level for the United Kingdom and a $2,468 million reserve level for France. These figures may be compared with the $5 billion reserve level often mentioned as a target by the British in past convertibility discussions, and with the $2.1 billion reserve level actually reached by France in the closing months of 1955.

Even at the 3 per cent growth rate assumed by the Fund's study, prospective gold supplies from new production and USSR sales would cover only 55 per cent of liquidity requirements over the ten years 1958–67. This proportion would drop to 43 per cent at a 4 per cent growth rate, 35 per cent at a 5 per cent growth rate and 29 per cent at a 6 per cent growth rate. The maintenance of adequate reserve levels, under the above assumptions, would thus require increases of gold production, decreases in gold hoarding, or supplementary reserve supplies in forms other than gold, ranging from roughly $6 billion to $17 billion over the next ten years.

Prospective Supplies of Monetary Gold

The Fund's estimate of a $7 billion increase in gold reserves over the next ten years rests on far more solid grounds than its estimate of future reserve requirements. It is based on a previous and excellent staff study[3] whose main conclusions are summarized in the first three columns of Table 9.

These estimates appear reasonable in the light of past experience. The probable value assigned to non-monetary uses of gold appears high at first view, but no longer does so when compared to past ex-

3. Oscar L. Altman, "A Note on Gold Production and Additions to International Gold Reserves," IMF *Staff Papers*, April 1958, pp. 258–288.

perience—outside the period of large-scale dishoarding which followed the revaluation of gold in the early 1930's[4]—if one takes into account the enormous increase in world incomes which has taken place since 1928. The figure given for artistic and industrial uses

TABLE 9

Supplies and Uses of Gold: 1890-1957 and Forecasts, 1958-1967

(Yearly Averages, expressed in millions of U.S. dollars at $35 an ounce)

	Forecast 1958-67			Past Averages						
	Pessi-mistic	Opti-mistic	Prob-able	1952-1957	1945-1951	1939-1944	1934-1938	1929-1933	1914-1928	1890-1913
1. New Production[1]	1050	1150	1100	940	800	1090	970	780	670	520
2. USSR Sales . .	—[2]	200[2]	100	105	10	30	−10	—	—	—
3. Total Supplies (1+2=4+5) . .	1050	1350	1200	1045	810	1120	960	780	670	520
4. Non-Monetary Uses[1]	660	330	470	495	440	−70	−310	480	280	220
a. Arts and Industry . . .	210	130	170	185	180	100	100	100	140	130
b. Hoarding . .	450	200	300	310	260	−170	−410	380	140	90
5. Monetary Uses[1]	390[2]	1020[2]	730	550	370	1190	1270	300	390	300

Footnotes: 1. USSR included before 1934.

2. Altman's study estimates USSR sales at $100 million throughout, and gives therefore a narrower range — $500 million to $920 million — for forecast additions to monetary gold.

Sources: These rough estimates have been pieced together from the following sources:

a. the International Monetary Fund: Altman's study quoted above; *International Reserves and Liquidity;* and the January 1959 issue of *International Financial Statistics.*

b. the statistical tables regularly published in the *Federal Reserve Bulletin,* and the article on *The Private Demand for Gold* in the September 1954 issue of the same Bulletin, pp. 935-944.

c. the estimates on private demand for gold, regularly published since the war in the *Annual Reports* of the Bank for International Settlements; and in the *Eighth Annual Report* (May 1938, p. 45) for the period 1931-1937.

d. the *Annual Report of the Secretary of the Treasury* for the fiscal year ended June 30, 1954, p. 294.

e. the various reports issued by the Gold Delegation of the Financial Committee of the League of Nations; and particularly in its *Interim Report* (1930), pp. 79-84, 90-94, and 114-117.

seems indeed exceedingly modest in the light of the League of Nations' estimates for the period 1891–1928. Overall non-monetary absorption ranged from 40 to 60 per cent of total production in every decade from 1850 to 1929. Mr. Altman himself suggests (p. 287)

4. See below, pp. 52–53.

that from one third to one half of gold production may continue to be so absorbed in the future. Applied to the production forecasts of Table 9, this would put non-monetary absorption within a range of $380 million to $525 million, and the amounts left for monetary uses between $525 million and $970 million, with a probable value of maybe $750 million.

The most vulnerable part of these forecasts is that referring to USSR gold sales to the West. All estimates of USSR gold stocks, gold production and gold sales are, of course, highly conjectural. Mr. Altman quotes estimates of $7 billion for stocks, and of $600 million for current production in 1957. Even more conjectural is the course of future USSR policy with respect to gold sales in world markets. An aggressive use of Russia's gold resources to serve political or economic objectives would, of course, play havoc with all estimates regarding the prospective adequacy of future gold reserves.

Finally, a word may be added about another, equally conjectural hypothesis, *i.e.* the possible dishoarding of gold privately accumulated in the past. The study on *International Reserves and Liquidity* quotes (p. 66), without sources, estimates of private gold hoards "of the order of $10 to $12 billion, of which one half is held in Western Europe, and almost one third in France alone." Such estimates can only be pulled from a magician's hat, the magician being in this case the well-known gold and exchange note publicist, Mr. Franz Pick.[5] This estimate may be compared with those pieced together in Table 10 from more official sources, and which suggest a figure of about $21 billion for "disappeared gold," but of only $8 billion for private gold hoards. The highly conjectural nature of these estimates, however, especially for the earlier years, deprives them of any real significance for policy. The cumulative estimates for gold hoarding in recent years are probably somewhat better, although still very far from reliable. They would suggest an increase of gold hoards of the order of $3 billion to $4 billion between 1913 and 1933, a decrease of about $3 billion between 1933 and 1944, and an increase of approximately $4 billion between 1944 and 1957.

A new wave of dishoarding, similar to that of the 1930's might possibly reduce somewhat the prospective gap between gold production and reserve requirements over the next ten years. The total amount that could realistically be expected from this source, however, would be small at best. The only case on record in the past is that of the 1930's, triggered off by a major depression and by drastic

5. See Mr. Altman's article, p. 286, footnote 57.

TABLE 10

Gold Supply and Uses, 1493-1957

(in billions of dollars, at $35 per ounce)

| | | | Other Uses | | | Cumulative Amounts, at End of Period | | | | |
| | | | | | | | | Disappeared Gold | | |
	Pro-duction	Mon-etary Uses	Total	Arts and Indus-try	Hoard-ing	Gold Stock	Mon-etary Gold	Total	Arts and Indus-try	Hoard-ing
1493–1849	5.2	1.8	3.4	2.6	0.8	5.2	1.8	3.4	5.2	1.8
1850–1869	4.3	2.7	1.6	0.9	0.7	9.5	4.5	5.0	3.6	1.5
1870–1889	3.7	1.4	2.3	1.8	0.5	13.2	5.9	7.3	5.4	2.0
1890–1913	12.5	7.2	5.4	3.2	2.2	25.7	13.0	12.7	8.6	4.1
1914–1928	10.0	5.8	4.2	2.1	2.0	35.7	18.8	16.9	10.7	6.2
1929–1933	3.9	1.5	2.4	0.5	1.9	39.6	20.3	19.3	11.2	8.1
Excluding USSR and other Eastern Europe, but including USSR Gold Sales						36.9	19.6	17.3	10.1	7.2
1934–1938	4.8	6.3	−1.5	0.5	−2.0	41.7	25.9	15.8	10.6	5.2
1939–1944	6.7	7.1	−0.4	0.6	−1.0	48.5	33.1	15.4	11.2	4.2
1945–1951	5.7	2.6	3.1	1.3	1.8	54.1	35.7	18.5	12.5	6.0
1952–1957	6.3	3.3	3.0	1.2	1.8	60.4	39.0	21.4	13.7	7.8

Notes: Sources for these highly conjectural estimates are given above, under Table 9. Post-1934 estimates are based on Federal Reserve, IMF and BIS reports and are probably reasonably accurate, except for the breakdown of "other uses," and for the *cumulative* estimates of production and "disappeared gold." These depend on a rough link over the years 1928-33 with previous estimates of the Gold Delegation of the League of Nations and on the validity of these estimates with respect to gold production for earlier years. Russian gold output up to the end of 1929 was estimated by Kitchin at £389 million (*Interim Report of the Gold Delegation*, p. 56), or about $3.2 billion in present day dollars, while our table would imply a figure of only $2.7 billion up to the end of 1933. Monetary gold estimates for earlier years include highly uncertain estimates for gold in circulation outside Central Banks and Treasuries. The figures given in the source for pre-1930 gold hoardings refer to gold hoardings in India, China and Egypt.

and widespread currency devaluations. Other solutions to the gold shortage problem would certainly seem to be highly desirable.

The Role of Foreign Exchange Reserves

Foreign exchange holdings have become, in recent years, a far larger source of current additions to world liquidity than gold itself. The Fund's study on *International Reserves and Liquidity* (pp. 72–73) recalls that "all short-term dollar balances in the last decade . . . increased on the average by $770 million per year, and official balances alone increased by $650 million per year. Sterling balances in the past decade have naturally been reduced from the swollen heights they attained by the end of World War II. . . . When all kinds of exchange holdings are taken together, the available data suggest that these reserves increased by a net total of about $2 billion in the past decade, or by $200 million per year."

These facts are not in doubt, and confirm indeed the view that gold has long ceased to provide an adequate supply of international

TABLE 11
Sources of Increase in Monetary Reserves Outside
the United States, 1950-1957

	In millions of US dollars	In % of total
Total Increase, from:	**10,936**	**100**
1. *Decrease in US Net Reserves:*	*6,851*	*63*
a) Decrease in Gold Assets	1,706	16
b) Increase in Dollar Reserve Liabilities	5,145	47
2. *Increase in World's Gold Reserves*	*3,915*	*36*
a) New Gold Production Outside Soviet Bloc	7,342	67
b) USSR Sales	635	6
c) Non-Monetary Absorption (—)	— 4,062	— 37
3. *Other*	*170*	*1*
a) Sterling Balances	— 1,578	— 14
b) Claims on EPU-BIS	1,570	14
c) Increase in International Organizations' Gold Assets (—)	— 80	— 1
d) Other and Errors	258	2

Sources: 1. Gold production and gold reserves are taken or calculated from *Federal Reserve Bulletin* estimates, and USSR sales from the *Annual Reports* of the Bank for International Settlements.
2. All other estimates are calculated from estimates in the January 1959 issue of *International Financial Statistics* (p. 17) and from *International Reserves and Liquidity* (p. 103).

liquidity for an expanding world economy. More than half of the world's liquidity requirements have been derived in recent years from the enormous growth of foreign exchange reserves, and particularly of dollar balances, alongside of gold itself. The implications of this trend for the future stability of the world monetary system are, however, extremely disquieting.

The increase of monetary reserves outside the United States has roughly kept pace, since the end of 1949, with the expansion of these countries' trade. Their growth over the eight years 1950–1957 has proceeded at an average rate of about 5½ per cent a year, *i.e.* close to the maximum rate envisaged in Table 8, above. Of this overall increase of $10.9 billion, however, a little more than a third (36 per cent) was fed from current gold production and USSR sales, and nearly two thirds (63 per cent) was derived from a continuous decline in the United States net reserves.

This decline, in turn, did not, until very recently, give rise to any serious concern. First of all, the United States had emerged from the war with extremely high reserves, largely in excess of any con-

TABLE 12

Proportions of Gold and Foreign Exchange to Total Monetary Reserves
Outside the United States and the United Kingdom, 1913-1957

(in per cent)

	Gold	*Foreign Exchange*			
		Total	*Dollar*	*Sterling*	*BIS-EPU*
1913	84	16			
1928	62	38			
1932	87	13			
1937	79	21			
1938	82	18	5	13	
1947	35	65	8	57	
1948	33	67	13	53	
1949	41	59	15	42	1
1950	39	61	19	37	2
1951	41	59	18	35	4
1952	41	59	22	28	6
1953	41	59	24	28	7
1954	41	59	26	27	6
1955	42	58	28	24	5
1956	43	57	29	22	5
1957	45	55	27	21	6

Sources: See Table 14, pp. 72-73.

ceivable need. A more even distribution of world reserves was regarded as a necessary step toward the restoration of a viable system of international convertibility. Secondly, only a small portion of the United States loss of net reserves took the form of a drain on its gold holdings. These declined only by $1.7 billion, or about 7 per cent between the end of 1949 and the end of 1957. Foreign countries accumulated nearly half of their reserve increase in the form of dollar claims rather than of gold.[6]

6. The huge United States gold losses of 1958 have, since this was written, finally wakened public opinion to the dangers pointed out below, and to which I vainly tried to draw attention in the spring of 1957 (see *Europe and the Money Muddle,* pp. 296-298).

The question at issue is how long such a trend can be expected to continue. Past experience is not reassuring in this respect. Foreign exchange holdings—primarily pounds and dollars—constituted at the end of 1957 about 55 per cent of the monetary reserves of countries other than the United States and the United Kingdom. Such a ratio does not appear excessive with reference to previous post-war years. Indeed, a substantially higher ratio (67 per cent) prevailed at the end of 1948, but most of it (53 per cent) was then in the form of inconvertible, and even partly blocked, sterling balances which could not be regarded as international monetary reserves in the full sense of the word.

The growth of foreign exchange reserves during and after World War II repeated, but on a much larger scale, their similar expansion after the first world war. Foreign exchange reserves had then risen from an estimated $500 million (16 per cent of total reserves) in 1913 to $3250 million (38 per cent of reserves) in 1928. This trend was encouraged by the international monetary conference of Genoa, in the spring of 1922, as a remedy to the shortage of gold. It was also propagandized throughout the 1920's by the United Kingdom, whose very low reserve position was considerably eased by foreign accumulation of sterling balances. The British return to convertibility in 1925 was thus assisted to a great degree by the maintenance of short-term balances by foreign countries in the London market.

This, however, also made the British position highly vulnerable as these short-term funds could move in and out under the stimulus of changes in relative interest rates in different monetary centers—particularly between London and New York—and of changes of expectations regarding the future evolution of exchange rates between London and other places.

The need to retain short-term funds in London by keeping higher discount rates in London than in New York was generally endorsed by Governor Strong of the Federal Reserve Bank of New York, and by the Governor of the Bank of England, Montagu Norman, but repeatedly gave rise to serious conflicts with other policy criteria in both countries. Unemployment and depressed levels of economic activity in England stimulated a clamor for easier credit policies, while credit restrictions were advocated in the United States as a necesary brake upon stock market speculation.[7]

7. See Lester V. Chandler, *Benjamin Strong, Central Banker*, Brookings Institute, 1958, Chapter VIII, pp. 291–331.

A temporary euphoria resulted, moreover, from the outflow of hot money from the continent during the years of currency depreciation of the mid-1920's. The reversal of this movement was well-nigh unavoidable at some point and created enormous embarrassment in London, particularly when the French franc began its spectacular recovery from 260 francs to the pound to 125 francs, after the accession to power of the Poincaré government. The Bank of France had to buy pounds massively from the market to slow down, and finally arrest, the appreciation of the franc. The partial conversion of these balances into gold and dollars began the hemorrhage of reserves from London. The final blow came in the summer of 1931, when the development of the world crisis put into difficulties the Credit Anstalt of Vienna, triggering a financial panic which spread rapidly throughout Central Europe and led to further and massive withdrawals of funds from London.

The devaluation of the pound, on September 21, 1931, sounded the knell of the gold exchange standard. The conversion of pounds into gold and dollars was accompanied and followed by similar conversions of dollars into gold. The foreign exchange component of the world's monetary reserves was nearly wiped out in the process, except for the countries of the sterling area. Dollar balances—official and private—fell from $2.7 billion in 1929 to less than $0.4 billion at the end of 1933.

Substantial exchange losses were experienced at that time, and once again in 1949, particularly by sterling holders. Some of the central banks concerned were reimbursed by special legislation, but saw their management sharply criticized in the course of the parliamentary debates to which this gave rise. This experience has not been forgotten and is likely to act as a brake on further accumulation of foreign exchange reserves beyond the swollen levels which they have already reached. Any drop in the interest rates available on such short term balances, or any impairment of confidence in the future stability of the center countries' currencies, would slow down further the accumulation of foreign exchange balances by central banks, and might even stimulate substantial conversions of existing balances into gold.

It seems most unlikely, therefore, that the growth of dollar or sterling balances can provide a lasting solution to the inadequacy of gold production to satisfy prospective requirements for international liquidity in an expanding world economy. The problem has been postponed in this manner after World War II, exactly as it was after World War I. Time, however, is running short, and the danger is increasing daily that further inaction and complacency may lead to a repetition, in a different form, of the 1931 collapse of the gold exchange standard.

Before coming to such a conclusion, however, we should now turn to a brief examination of the reserve position of the two center countries of the present international monetary system, *i.e.* the United Kingdom and the United States.

CHAPTER 6

The Position of the Center Countries

The United Kingdom and Its Sterling Balances

Sterling balances made up, at the end of the war, the overwhelming bulk of official foreign exchange holdings. They reached, according to the Fund's estimates,[1] the equivalent of $12.1 billion at the end of 1947, *i.e.* 88 per cent of total official foreign exchange balances, as against 12 per cent for official dollar balances.

Total sterling balances, official and private, exceeded $14 billion, *i.e.* about 288 per cent of the United Kingdom's annual exports. Such huge balances would not, of course, have been accumulated during the war, and retained after the war, without a considerable element of compulsion. Large amounts of them were blocked by British regulations, and other holdings were subject to various degrees of restrictions on their use, ranging from full convertibility —but at the cost of severe import restrictions—for the insignificantly low balances held in the dollar area, to purely bilateral accounts in the case of countries outside the sterling and the transferable area systems.

The dismal failure of the brief 1947 convertibility experiment amply demonstrated the need for a substantial reduction—rather than further expansion—of sterling balances. The spectacular progress achieved in this direction in the following ten years was a clear prerequisite for another, and less ephemeral, return to convertibility.

1. See, however, p. 37 above. Official sterling holdings at the end of 1945 were reported in *Economic Trends* (May 1958, p. viii) as equivalent to about $11 billion inclusive of British colonies, and $10 billion if colonies are excluded. No comparable figures are available for 1947. The total of sterling balances—official and private— declined only slightly—by about $280 million—between these two years, a total reduction of approximately $520 million in private and official holdings outside the British colonies being partly offset by the concomitant increase ($240 million) in colonial holdings.

Measured in sterling terms, the overall reduction is extremely modest. Total territorial sterling balances fell only from 3.5 billion pounds in 1947 to about 3.3 billion pounds in 1958. Moreover, a substantial portion of this decline is offset by increased sterling holdings of IMF and EPU, and by other short or medium term official British borrowings in the United States.

The improvement must indeed be measured in other ways. The actual burden of the sterling balances was, first of all, greatly reduced in dollar and in commodity terms by the sterling devaluation of 1949 and by a rise of more than 50 per cent in British export prices. The simultaneous expansion of nearly 80 per cent in the volume of British exports has also increased the normal demand for sterling balances. Thirdly, sterling balances held outside the sterling area have been more than halved, even in sterling terms, the largest part of this decline being accounted for, however, by a considerable increase in the more easily controllable holdings of colonial territories.

All in all, sterling balances today bear about the same relation to British exports as they did in 1938, and those held outside the sterling area represent only 22 per cent of annual imports, as against 44 per cent in 1938. Official balances of non-sterling countries were estimated in 1957 at less than $850 million, compared to more than $3.2 billion at the end of 1945.

Confidence in sterling has also increased considerably with other, and multiplying, signs of Britain's postwar recovery. The most striking of these are the increase in the United Kingdom's gold and dollar reserves since the end of 1957, and the large and growing surpluses on current account displayed by the balance of payments in 1957 ($0.9 billion) and in 1958 ($1.5 billion).

It is not unlikely, therefore, that the forthcoming months may witness a considerable demand for sterling balances by foreign countries. Sterling balances of non-sterling countries had indeed increased already by $456 million (28 per cent) in 1958, before the impact of the convertibility decisions of the end of the year could be felt.

Further increases may be expected as a result of two features of the European Monetary Agreement which have not received all the attention which they deserve from economists and financial analysts. The first is that all OEEC countries are now free to accumulate sterling reserves if they so wish, while they were debarred

TABLE 13

The Reserve Position of the Center Countries, 1928-1958

	1928	1932	1938	1947	1949	1953	1957	1958
I. The United States								
A. Gold Reserves ($billions) .	4.1	4.0	14.6	22.9	24.6	22.1	22.9	20.6
B. Dollar Balances ($billions)	2.5	0.7	2.2	7.1	8.2	12.7	16.6	17.6
1. International . . .	—	—	—	2.3	1.8	1.9	1.7	2.0
2. Countries: . . .	2.5	0.7	2.2	4.9	6.4	10.8	14.9	15.6
a. Official[1] . . .			0.5	1.8	3.4	6.5	9.1	9.6
b. Private			1.7	3.0	3.1	4.4	5.7	6.0
C. Ratio of Dollar Balances (excl. International) to U.S. Exports (in per cent)	48	44	71	32	53	68	72	87
1. Official[1]			16	12	28	41	44	54
2. Private			55	19	26	28	27	33
D. Ratio of Total Dollar Balances to U.S. Gold Reserves (in per cent)	61	17	15	31	33	57	72	86
II. The United Kingdom								
A. Gold and Dollar Reserves ($billions)	0.7	0.6	2.9	2.2	1.8	2.5	2.4	3.1
B. Sterling Balances ($billions)[2]	2.4	1.4	2.8	15.7	10.4	11.2	10.9	11.1
1. International . . .	—	—	—	1.6	1.6	1.4	1.8	1.7
2. Countries . . .	2.4	1.4	2.8	14.1	8.8	9.8	9.2	9.4
a. Colonies . . .		} 0.7	} 1.6	1.9	1.5	3.1	2.5	2.5
b. Other Sterling Area				7.2	4.5	4.8	5.1	4.9
c. Non-Sterling Area		0.7	1.2	5.0	2.7	1.9	1.6	2.0
(1) OEEC . . .				1.7	1.0	0.6	0.7	1.0
(2) Other . .				3.3	1.8	1.3	0.9	1.0
C. Ratio of Sterling Balances (excl. International) to U.K. Exports (in per cent) . . .	69	108	104	288	127	131	94	100
1. Colonies		} 54	} 59	39	22	41	26	26
2. Other Sterling Area				147	65	64	53	52
3. Non-Sterling Area .		54	44	102	39	25	16	22
a. OEEC				35	14	8	7	11
b. Other				67	25	17	9	11
D. Ratio of Total Sterling Balances to U.K. Gold and Dollar Reserves . .	320	240	95	705	595	440	460	360

Footnotes: 1. Official dollar balances include small amounts of "bonds and notes," reported only since 1949 and for which no breakdown is available between official and private holdings.

2. Sterling balance estimates for 1928 are from the (Macmillan) *Committee on Finance and Industry Report* (London, 1931), pp. 42 and 301. Those for 1932 are from the BIS study on *The Sterling Area* (Basle, 1953) and actually refer to the end of 1931. The 1938 estimate is taken from the *Twenty Second Annual Report* of the BIS (Basle, 1952), p. 172. These are probably fairly rough estimates, not fully comparable with postwar estimates.

from doing this under the monthly compensation machinery of the EPU Agreement. The second is that such holdings will enjoy a firm exchange guarantee in terms of the U.S. dollar, under Article 11 of the European Monetary Agreement, while dollar holdings will not benefit from any similar guarantee in terms of sterling. Although any devaluation of the dollar with relation to sterling may now appear as a very remote and improbable contingency, this difference of treatment should not be entirely forgotten. More immediately significant, however, is the fact that European central banks are now free to accumulate sterling, if they so choose, without taking any exchange risk in the case of a devaluation of sterling with respect to the dollar. A substantial lowering of interest rates in New York compared to London might thus easily induce considerable shifts of short-term balances from dollar to sterling assets.

In spite of this, little reliance should be placed on the future growth of sterling balances to fill the prospective gap between gold production and world reserve requirements.

The main reason for this is that gross British reserves are still very low in relation to short-term sterling liabilities. The difficulties repeatedly encountered by Britain, for that very reason, in 1931, 1947, 1949, 1951, 1953 and 1957 are likely to induce her to match any increase in sterling balances by equivalent, or more than equivalent, increases in her own reserve assets. Little net additions to world liquidity should, therefore, be expected from this source.

The United States and Its Dollar Balances

The prospective growth of dollar balances offers, at first view, more promising possibilities. In spite of their enormous increase since the war, dollar balances still do not appear excessive in relation to United States exports. The ratio of the first to the latter (87 per cent) is only slightly larger than in 1938, and still well below the corresponding ratio for the United Kingdom (100 per cent). In sharp contrast to the British case, moreover, our gold stock is still substantially larger than our total short-term liabilities abroad.

It is indeed the persistent decline in our net reserve position which has been, by far, the major source of supply for the very satisfactory growth of other countries' reserves since 1949.[2] This fact received little public notice as long as the drain on our reserves took the form of an increase in our short-term dollar liabilities

2. See above, pp. 53–55 and Table 11.

abroad rather than in a loss of gold from Fort Knox. From 1949 to the end of 1957, our gold stock decreased only by $1.7 billion, or about 7 per cent, while our dollar liabilities more than doubled, from $8.2 billion to $16.6 billion.

This rapid growth of dollar balances during the postwar years reflected, at least in part, the substitution of convertible dollars for inconvertible sterling in world settlements and world reserves. This throws further doubt on the likelihood of any continued and indefinite accumulation of dollar balances abroad on a scale comparable to that experienced during the last decade. The prediction which I had ventured in this respect in the spring of 1957 [3] seemed to find some confirmation in 1958. In the course of that year, foreign countries' short-term dollar holdings—including bonds and notes—rose only by $700 million, while net gold purchases from the United States totalled $2,300 million.

The United States gold losses of 1958 are beginning to create some concern about the continued deterioration in the country's net reserve position. The excess of gold reserves over short-term liabilities to foreign countries—including bonds and notes—has declined continually from $18.2 billion at the end of 1949 to less than $5 billion at the end of 1958, i.e. at an annual rate of more than $1.3 billion over the years 1950–1957, and by nearly $3 billion in 1958 alone.

Such a movement obviously could not continue indefinitely without ultimately undermining foreigners' confidence in the dollar as a safe medium for reserve accumulation. The time will certainly come, sooner or later, when further accumulation of short-term foreign liabilities will either have to be slowed down or substantially matched by corresponding increases in our already bloated gold assets. If this were not done on our own initiative, foreign central banks would do it for us by stopping their own accumulation of dollar assets and requiring gold payment instead for their overall surplus with the United States.

As in the case of sterling balances, therefore, further increases in dollar balances cannot be relied upon to contribute substantially and indefinitely to the solution of the world illiquidity problem.

3. *Europe and the Money Muddle*, p. 297.

CHAPTER 7

The Gold Exchange Standard

Before discussing other possible remedies, it may be advisable to broaden our understanding of the problem by inserting it into a larger historical context. The problem indeed is not new, although it has manifested itself in many different forms in past history, and been solved in a great variety of ways.

It is not necessary to accept any rigid version of the quantity theory of money to recognize that some link has always existed between monetary expansion and economic growth. The link is a loose one, and does not in any way imply a simple causal relationship. Monetary expansion will not automatically ensure economic growth. It may, however, stimulate it. What is even clearer, and more relevant to the present discussion, is that economic growth is almost certain to be arrested or slowed down at some point if the way cannot be found to ensure a parallel—although by no means proportionate—increase in monetary liquidity.

Previous to the large-scale development of banking institutions in the nineteenth century, gold and silver remained for many centuries the main source of supply of new money in the West. Their relative abundance or scarcity could not fail to play an important—although neither decisive nor exclusive—role in the evolution of prices and of economic activity. Every economic historian has stressed, for instance, the impact exercised in this respect by the influx of gold and silver into Spain and into Europe following the discovery of America. Long waves of economic activity in the nineteenth century—the so-called Kondratieff cycles—have similarly been related by many economists to the uneven pace of gold discoveries and production. Economists, however, are prone to stress the originality, rather than the conformism, of their views, and to emphasize the differences of interpretation that distinguish them from their colleagues, rather than the common ground on which they would all meet. Their basic agreement on the points mentioned above is thus often veiled by controversies over the relative weight to be given, in the analysis of events, to monetary and real factors, and over the "causal" direction which runs between the first and the latter. We are here, however, looking at the forest rather than at the trees, and these differences do not invalidate the broad conclusion that a lag in monetary expansion may act at times—and often has acted in the past—as a brake on the rate of economic development.

For many centuries, the repeated debasement of coinage constituted the main escape from the difficulties resulting from the failure of gold and silver supplies to keep pace with the monetary needs of individual countries.[4] The stability exhibited by the major Western currencies with respect to gold throughout the nineteenth century was unprecedented in history. It was largely the product of an enormous expansion in gold production and of the large-scale development of paper currency and deposit-money as adjuncts to gold and silver in monetary transactions.

These new forms of money, however, were now national, rather than international, and the maintenance of exchange rate stability became dependent on their convertibility into internationally acceptable money by the issuing institution. The incidence of this on the problem of international reserves has already been traced in the earlier sections of this study. All that we need observe at this stage is the economy in the use of scarce gold supplies which was effected by the gradual shift of gold coin from circulation in the public to the reserves of the banking system and, later on, from private circulation and bank reserves to the reserves of a single national institution, i.e. the Treasury or Central Bank. The latter phenomenon was one of the three major remedies applied to the shortage of gold reserves in relation to the vastly expanded circulation of national paper money and bank deposits during and after the first world war. Gold reserves nearly doubled between 1913 and 1928, passing from $4.9 to $10.0 billion—including Russian gold—but of this total increase of $5.1 billion less than half ($2.3 billion) was derived from the excess of new gold production over non-monetary absorption, and about 55 per cent ($2.8 billion) from the contraction of monetary gold outside Treasuries and Central Banks.

---

4. The gold content of the French "livre tournois" gradually fell, for instance, from about 3.2 grams of fine gold in 1351 to 0.29 grams in 1795, i.e. a debasement of more than 90 per cent. The fine gold content of British coinage fell somewhat less, by 77 per cent, between 1257 and 1816. See Chart III, p. 80.

The second remedy lay in the drastic devaluation of many currencies with respect to gold, and to the consequent revaluation of gold reserves in terms of national currencies.

These two categories of measures did not succeed in restoring fully the prewar proportion of gold reserves to the currency issues and other sight liabilities of central banks. The ratio of the first to the latter dropped from 48 per cent in 1913 to about 40 per cent in the late 1920's.[5]

The third remedy resorted to during this period was, as already noted in previous chapters, a much wider reliance on national key currencies—primarily sterling and dollars—as additional components of world monetary reserves. By combining the above estimates with the IMF estimates of foreign exchange reserves ($500 million in 1913 and $3,250 million in 1928) one arrives at a ratio of total reserves to sight liabilities of 53 to 54 per cent, both in 1913 and 1928.

Such world averages, however, concealed wide variations in the reserve position of individual countries. Approximately half of the world's reserves were concentrated in 1928 in two countries only, France and the United States, while the gold reserves of the Bank of England ($750 million) were less than a fourth of sterling deposits and bills held or accepted in London on foreign account.[6]

The increasing use of foreign exchange balances as a remedy to world illiquidity under the new gold exchange standard had thus fatally weakened the reserve position of the country on which the system was primarily dependent for its continued operation. The collapse of the major key currency of the system in 1931 inevitably sucked other currencies into the whirlpool, and entailed the temporary breakdown, not only of sterling, but of the international monetary system itself.

An unprecedented degree of international liquidity was nevertheless reached in the 1930's, in spite of the near-disappearance of the foreign exchange component of world reserves. This, however, came as the by-product of widespread currency devaluation and,

5. *Interim Report of the Gold Delegation of the Financial Committee* (League of Nations, Geneva, 1930), p. 94.

6. Expressed in pounds sterling, the gold reserves of the Bank of England at the end of 1928 were about £154 million. Deposits and sterling bills held in London on foreign account—including advances to the discount market—totalled £500 million. Acceptances on foreign account totalled another £200 million. See the (Macmillan) *Committee on Finance and Industry Report,* London, 1931, p. 301.

most of all, of a drastic and prolonged contraction in the volume and value of world trade. Deflation, devaluation and restrictions were the three sources of the unwanted levels of international monetary liquidity of the 1930's. They also reflected, at least in part, the vulnerability imparted by the gold *exchange* standard to the monetary centers of the system and transmitted through them to the world monetary system itself.

The basic absurdity of the gold exchange standard is that it makes the *international* monetary system highly dependent on individual countries' decisions about the continued use of one or a few *national* currencies as monetary reserves. In the absence of any widespread doubts about exchange rate stability, the choice of such currencies as reserves normally falls on the currencies of the countries which play a major role in world trade and finance. Sterling, the dollar and, subsidiarily, the French franc thus became the main reserve currencies in the 1920's. When doubts about the future stability of exchange rates begin to develop, however, the weaker currencies quickly tend to be eliminated from this competition, and the choice of reserve currencies narrows down to the strongest, hardest, and thus safest, currencies in world trade and settlements. When even these begin to be questioned, a further shift to gold may bring the gold exchange standard to an end and move the work back toward the previous gold, or gold bullion, standard.

The gold exchange standard *may*, but *does not necessarily*, help in relieving a shortage of world monetary reserves. It does so only to the extent that the key currency countries are willing to let their net reserve position decline through increases in their short-term monetary liabilities unmatched by corresponding increases in their own gross reserves. If they allow this to happen, however, and to continue indefinitely, they tend to bring about a collapse of the system itself through the gradual weakening of foreigners' confidence in the key currencies.

This happened to the United Kingdom in 1931. The collapse was then brought about by large shifts of sterling balances into gold and dollars, leading to the devaluation of sterling. It happened again as a consequence of wartime developments and resulted then both in the 1949 devaluation and in the protracted inconvertibility of sterling and recurring balance of payments crises of Britain throughout the postwar years.

This explains the division of views which has developed in

68 PART ONE: DIAGNOSIS

recent years in the United Kingdom about the relative advantages and disadvantages flowing to its own economy from the wide use of sterling as an international currency.[7] It may also help explain why other countries, such as Switzerland and Germany, have so far discouraged, rather than welcomed, the use of their national currency as international reserves.

The weakening of the sterling position, and of other major world currencies, after World War II concentrated the choice of all countries upon the United States dollar as the hardest, and thus safest, medium for the investment of their foreign exchange reserves. It carried coals to Newcastle in the form of "unrequited" lending by the rest of the world to the main creditor country. This added to the difficulties which the United States already confronted in developing a sufficient level of *net* capital exports to finance its large surpluses on current account and avoid an aggravation of the dollar shortage.

To the extent that we succeeded in doing this, however, we also tended, inevitably, to adjust our overall balance of payments on current and U.S. capital account—including official grants and loans—to the persistent inflow of foreign short-term balances into our market, and to weaken correspondingly our net reserve position to a point beyond which neither we, nor probably foreign countries, would wish to venture much further. As we have already seen, the mere slowdown of this foreign capital inflow resulted in 1958 in a relatively large gold outflow. If the latter persists, or reasserts itself at a later date, we shall have to undertake some complex readjustments in our economic policies, in order to restore long-run equilibrium in our international transactions.

The relatively small role of external transactions in relation to GNP, and the enormous strength and resiliency of our economy, should facilitate these necessary readjustments, and rule out difficulties of the kind previously encountered by Britain. Only an incredible complacency on our part could bring us to the point where the weakening of our reserve position might finally stimulate massive conversions of foreign countries' existing dollar balances into gold, and force us to suspend or modify the legal gold cover requirements of the Federal Reserve System. Even this could, in any case, be done easily if economic considerations did not risk,

7. See particularly A.C.L. Day, *The Future of Sterling*, Oxford University Press. 1958.

at that stage, to be overshadowed by irrational, but powerful, psychological and political forces. Is it too fanciful to imagine that the Daughters of the American Revolution might then clamor for an embargo on gold sales or shipments abroad, and that the threat of any such action might precipitate the conversion of existing dollar balances into gold and force the authorities to resort to such drastic and calamitous measures, no matter how unnecessary these would have been in a calmer environment? A gold embargo would, however, entail nearly inevitably—even if only temporarily—a *de facto* depreciation of the dollar with respect to gold. Other currencies would probably find themselves involved in the process, as any expectations of a dollar depreciation in relation to gold would almost certainly be accompanied by expectations of a similar depreciation of other currencies, and would prompt legal or illegal flights into gold or real assets, abroad even more than in the United States.

I do not wish to suggest that such dramatic developments are in the least probable. They are, on the contrary, totally unlikely to occur. The United States authorities are well aware of the problem and determined to tackle it long before the danger point is reached. The real danger which we face is not that of a dollar collapse. It is the fact that such a collapse can ultimately be avoided only through a substantial slowdown of the contributions to world liquidity derived in the last nine years from the persistent weakening of our net reserve position. The solution of the dollar problem will thus involve a reopening or aggravation of the world liquidity problem.

Summary and Conclusions

The world's normal requirements for monetary reserves appropriate to the maintenance of convertibility by the major trading countries are likely to exceed considerably—by $5 billion to $15 billion —over the next ten years the contribution which may be expected for the purpose from current levels of gold production.[1]

This gap is unlikely to be filled by the supplementary contributions to world liquidity that may be derived from the further growth of dollar, sterling, and other national currency balances as media for reserve accumulation.

In the absence of any specific planning and policies, the growing inadequacy of world reserves would be most likely to lead, within a relatively short span of years, to a new cycle of international deflation, devaluation and restrictions, as it did after 1929. Such a cycle might possibly be triggered by unfavorable economic developments outside the center countries themselves, but its international spread would begin with the difficulties which the United States or the United Kingdom might experience as a result of any considerable slowdown or reversal of the inflow of foreign funds to their markets. The lessons of the 1930's and the radical changes which have taken place since then in governmental attitudes and policies would probably rule out any widespread recourse to, or acceptance of, internal deflation as a method of adjustment. Devaluation and restrictions would be the most likely outcome of such a situation.

Fortunately, a sufficient number of people are now alert to these dangers, and we have witnessed during the last year some modest

1. Including about $200 million a year of Russian gold sales to the West. The conclusions of this paper would, I must admit, be thoroughly upset if the USSR decided to use aggressively its vast gold stock in world markets, for economic or political purposes. Depending on the policies adopted on both sides of the famed iron curtain, this could either save or definitely wreck the gold standard as an international monetary mechanism.

beginnings toward advance planning in this field. The proposed expansion of the International Monetary Fund's quotas by 50 per cent, and of the International Bank's capital by 100 per cent are steps in the right direction. A less publicized, but important feature of the European Monetary Agreement is the exchange guarantee provided by it on all balances held by any participating country in the currency of any other participating country. This provision may indeed encourage a broader use of European currencies—and particularly sterling—as reserves by the countries concerned. Finally, the implementation of the provisions of the European Economic Community Treaty relating to coordination of economic and monetary policies and the adjustment of balances of payments within the Community may also lead to fruitful developments in the future.

Far more comprehensive measures than those adopted so far remain necessary, however, to adapt the old gold and gold exchange standards to the needs of our times and to provide the world with a viable framework for international payments in an expanding world economy. The most promising line of approach to a long-term solution of the problem lies in the true "internationalization" of the foreign exchange component of the world's international reserves, protecting the world monetary system from the instability resulting from arbitrary shifts from one reserve currency into another or into gold. Such a solution should be regarded as the normal culmination of one of the techniques used in the past to adjust the monetary system to the requirements of an expanding economy, *i.e.* the gradual withdrawal of gold coin from active circulation, and its concentration into the monetary reserves of national central banks. Its adoption can also develop only gradually at best, and premature or overambitious plans such as embodied in Keynes' famous *Proposals for an International Clearing Union* would be doomed to failure today, as they were in 1943.

It is to be hoped, however, that more modest and feasible agreements may prove negotiable in time, both regionally and internationally. Three institutions should normally take the lead in this respect: the International Monetary Fund, the Organization for European Economic Cooperation, and the European Economic Community. The probable scope and line of action of each will be discussed in Part Two of this book.

TABLE 14

Basic Estimates for Reserve Calculations, 1913-19[
(*in billions of U.S. dollars*)

	1913			1928			1932	1937	1938
	Re-serves	Gold Circu-lation	Total	Re-serves	Gold Circu-lation	Total			
I. *Gold*	4.03	3.26	7.29	9.76	0.75	10.51	11.35	25.31	25.95
A. United States . .	1.29	0.33	1.62	3.75	0.11	3.86	4.05	12.79	14.59
B. Other Countries .	2.74	2.93	5.68	6.01	0.64	6.65	7.30	12.52	11.36
1. United Kingdom	0.17	0.60	0.77	0.75	0.09	0.84	0.58	4.14	2.88
2. Other . . .	2.58	2.33	4.91	5.26	0.55	5.81	6.72	8.38	8.48
II. *Foreign Exchange* . .	0.50		0.50	3.25		3.25	1.00	2.26	1.80
A. United Kingdom .	—		—	—		—	—	—	—
1. Dollar . . .	—		—	—		—	—	—	—
2. EPU-BIS . .	—		—	—		—	—	—	—
3. Discrepancy .	—		—	—		—	—	—	—
B. Other Countries .	0.50		0.50	3.25		3.25	1.00	2.26	1.80
1. Dollar . . .									0.50
2. Sterling . . .									1.30
3. EPU-BIS . .									
4. Discrepancy .									
III. *Total*	4.53	3.26	7.79	13.01	0.75	13.76	12.35	27.57	27.75
A. United States . .	1.29	0.33	1.62	3.75	0.11	3.86	4.05	12.79	14.59
B. Other Countries .	3.24	2.93	6.18	9.26	0.64	9.90	8.30	14.78	13.16
1. United Kingdom	0.17	0.60	0.77	0.75	0.09	0.84	0.58	4.14	2.88
2. Other . . .	3.08	2.33	5.41	8.51	0.55	9.06	7.72	10.64	10.28
IV. *Imports*			21.0			30.6	12.71	27.62	23.54
A. United States . .			1.8			4.4	1.34	3.57	2.46
B. Other Countries .			19.2			26.2	11.37	24.05	21.07
1. United Kingdom			3.7			5.8	2.28	5.08	4.50
2. Other . . .			15.5			20.4	9.09	18.97	16.57
V. *Gross Reserve Ratio* (%) .	22	16	37	43	2	45	97	100	118
A. United States . .	72	18	90	85	3	88	302	358	592
B. Other Countries .	17	15	32	35	2	38	73	61	62
1. United Kingdom	5	16	21	13	1	14	26	81	64
2. Other . . .	20	15	35	42	3	44	85	55	62

Sources and Notes: Most of these estimates are derived from IMF gold, foreign exchange, and trade statistics, and exclude International Organizations and the Soviet Area countries.

International Financial Statistics' tables have been used for the years 1937 (February 1959 issue) and 1950-1958 (August 1959 issue); Appendix Table 3 of *International Reserves and Liquidity* for foreign exchange estimates for the years 1947-1949; and Appendix Table 2 of the same study for gold estimates for 1947-1949, and for both gold and foreign exchange estimates for 1938.

Other sources were used to check and complete the estimates for 1913, 1928, and particularly 1932. Preference was given for this purpose to the gold reserve statistics of the Federal Reserve *Banking and Monetary Statistics* (Washington, 1943), pp. 544-555, and to the estimates of gold circulation of the *Gold Delegation of the Financial Committee of the League*

1947	1948	1949	1950	1951	1952	1953	1954	1955	1956	1957	1958
32.40	32.75	33.15	33.83	33.94	33.95	34.37	34.98	35.46	36.10	37.36	38.07
22.87	24.40	24.56	22.82	22.87	23.25	22.09	21.79	21.75	22.06	22.86	20.58
9.53	8.35	8.59	11.01	11.07	10.70	12.28	13.19	13.71	14.04	14.50	17.49
2.02	1.60	1.35	2.90	2.20	1.50	2.30	2.55	2.05	1.80	1.60	2.85
7.51	6.75	7.24	8.11	8.87	9.20	9.98	10.64	11.66	12.24	12.90	14.64
13.90	13.90	10.85	13.84	13.33	13.77	14.83	15.86	16.36	17.02	16.54	16.55
0.21	0.40	0.40	0.77	0.17	0.46	0.25	0.25	0.11	0.37	0.77	0.26
0.06	0.25	0.34	0.40	0.13	0.35	0.22	0.21	0.07	0.33	0.67	0.22
—	—	—	0.23	—	—	—	—	—	—	—	—
0.15	0.15	0.06	0.14	0.04	0.11	0.03	0.04	0.04	0.04	0.10	0.04
13.69	13.50	10.45	13.07	13.16	13.31	14.58	15.61	16.25	16.65	15.77	16.29
1.79	2.65	2.71	4.04	3.87	4.90	5.79	6.85	7.80	8.23	7.52	8.26
12.15	10.77	7.41	7.92	7.83	6.52	7.03	7.30	6.93	6.56	6.14	6.77
—	0.05	0.11	0.42	0.86	1.44	1.62	1.57	1.41	1.51	1.68	2.24
-0.25	0.02	0.21	0.69	0.60	0.45	0.14	-0.10	0.11	0.35	0.43	-0.98
46.30	46.65	44.00	47.67	47.27	47.72	49.20	50.84	51.83	53.12	53.90	54.62
22.87	24.40	24.56	22.82	22.87	23.25	22.09	21.79	21.75	22.06	22.86	20.58
23.43	22.25	19.44	24.85	24.40	24.47	27.11	29.05	30.08	31.06	31.04	34.04
2.23	2.01	1.75	3.67	2.37	1.96	2.55	2.80	2.16	2.17	2.37	3.11
21.20	20.24	17.69	21.18	22.03	22.51	24.56	26.25	27.92	28.89	28.67	30.93
53.30	60.05	59.91	59.89	82.11	80.71	76.99	80.03	89.52	98.83	108.25	100.74
6.55	8.06	7.53	9.60	11.88	11.66	11.79	11.05	12.36	13.80	14.30	13.99
46.76	52.00	52.38	50.29	70.23	69.05	65.20	68.98	77.16	85.03	93.95	86.75
7.34	8.37	8.52	7.31	10.93	9.74	9.36	9.45	10.87	10.88	11.40	10.58
39.42	43.63	43.86	42.98	59.30	59.31	55.84	59.53	66.29	74.15	82.55	76.17
87	78	73	80	58	59	64	64	58	54	50	54
349	303	326	238	193	199	187	197	176	160	161	147
50	43	37	49	35	35	42	42	39	37	33	39
30	24	21	50	22	20	27	30	20	20	21	29
54	46	40	49	37	38	44	44	42	39	35	41

of Nations (1930 *Interim Report*, pp. 114-117 for 1913, and the 1932 *Report*, pp. 78-83 for 1928). Foreign exchange estimates for 1932 had to be pieced together from other League of Nations publications (particularly Ragnar Nurkse's *International Currency Experience*, League of Nations, 1944) and can only be regarded as a rough approximation.

Slight differences in the inclusiveness of estimates covering such an extended period of time are well-nigh unavoidable and introduce a corresponding margin of error in all calculations based on this Table, particularly for the years 1913-1949. *International Financial Statistics* began publishing in September 1959 slightly more comprehensive estimates of world monetary reserves since 1950. These would raise throughout by about 2 to 3 per cent the reserve ratios shown in this table and in the text, but would also make ₜhem even less comparable with estimates for earlier years.

Part Two

Prescription

Tomorrow's Convertibility: Aims and Means
of International Monetary Policy

Introduction

THE CONVERTIBILITY DECISIONS of December 1958 were both overdue and ill-prepared. They were long overdue in the light of the enormous and steady improvement of Europe's balance of payments position over the last decade. They were ill-prepared because they merely trusted to luck and neglected to build up any defenses against the most obvious dangers of an unorganized, nationalistic gold-exchange standard, so amply and catastrophically demonstrated by the rapid collapse of a similar "reconstruction" after the first world war.

Such was the gloomy theme of Part One of this book. Part Two will strike a more hopeful note by trying to explore some of the means by which the new convertibility could be given more solid foundations and contribute, at the same time, to a more rapid and balanced growth of the world economy.

Before venturing new and constructive suggestions in this respect, however, it is necessary to clear the air of two plausible, but illusory, solutions to the more immediate difficulties that may spring up within the next two or three years from the impending shortage of international reserves and liquidity.

The first—an upward revaluation of gold—is widely advocated and anticipated in "practical" financial circles, but finds very little audience in academic circles, with the outstanding exception of Sir Roy Harrod.

The second—freely fluctuating exchange rates—is, on the contrary, anathema to business opinion, but increasingly finds favor today with economic theorists—such as Professors Meade, Friedman, Haberler, etc.—as the miracle drug that will make international balance compatible with obdurately irresponsible national monetary and fiscal policies.

The reader who has remained blissfully impervious to either or both of these fallacious solutions to the world monetary problem will be well advised to skip my discussion of them in Chapter 1 and to turn directly to Chapter 2.

CHAPTER 1

Two False Solutions
to the World Liquidity Problem

A Revaluation of Gold

Although basically absurd, a drastic revaluation of current gold prices is by no means an unlikely solution to the world illiquidity problem. It will become well-nigh unavoidable—and far preferable indeed to the alternative solutions of world deflation or world restrictions—if international negotiation fails to develop in time other and more constructive solutions to the problem.

The stability of gold prices from the Napoleonic era to the first world war remains so far a unique exception in world history, explainable by the extraordinary development of national bank credit and paper money, on the one hand, and of gold production, on the other, in the nineteenth century.[1] The persistent upward trend of gold prices throughout history is dramatically illustrated in the accompanying Chart, reproduced from the 1951 Annual Report of the Bank for International Settlements (p. 157). The implication that "the current gold price, according to the trend of long history, would seem to be just right"[2] is, however, more specious than obvious, since very different conclusions would be drawn from similar charts of gold prices in terms of other major currencies. If "right" in terms of shillings, the gold price would, by the same reasoning, be far too high in terms of French francs, for instance, and far too low

1. Gold production is estimated to have risen from a yearly average of about 0.37 million ounces in the previous three centuries to 3.72 million ounces—or ten times as much—in the nineteenth century, and 19.23 million in the thirteen years preceding the first world war.

2. *Monthly Letter,* First National City Bank, February 1959, p. 23.

in terms of dollars. The only conclusions which might be retained from such historical records are:

1. that gold production has rarely kept pace, over the long run, with the monetary demand for gold arising from different, but nearly uniformly upward, trends in prices and economic activity in different countries;

2. that this gap has been met, throughout history, by differential

CHART III

Gold Price in London over Seven Centuries
(in shillings per fine ounce)

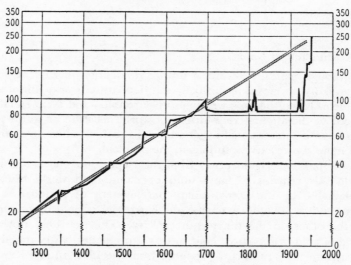

rates of currency debasement or devaluation in terms of gold, as well as by the expansion of other types of monetary instruments, particularly paper money and bank deposits; and

3. that this historical trend is likely to assert itself persistently in the long run, and to entail a continuous or periodic depreciation of national currencies in terms of gold, whenever alternative means are not found to provide an adequate supply of monetary liquidity —international as well as national—for an expanding world economy.

Such a result, however, is not unavoidable. It can be obviated if—

and this is admittedly a big IF—international negotiations and agreements can be substituted for *laissez faire* and inertia. The arguments against gold revaluation should be powerful enough to elicit a determined effort in this direction.

First of all, the increase in gold prices needed to stimulate adequate annual supplies of monetary gold would have to be very steep indeed. Such supplies would probably have to be doubled or tripled—in dollar terms—to meet the problem as appraised in Part One of this study.[3]

Secondly, this gold revaluation operation would have to be repeated at periodic intervals, in order to keep pace with the cumulative growth of the world economy.

Thirdly, each of these revaluations would result in a temporary excess of world liquidity, due to their impact upon the valuation of existing gold reserves at the time. A fifty per cent revaluation, for instance, would produce today an overnight increase of gold and foreign exchange reserves of nearly $20 billion for countries outside the Soviet bloc.

Fourthly, the benefits of gold revaluation would be distributed very haphazardly and, indeed, in just about the least desirable fashion imaginable. High reserve countries would benefit most, and low reserve countries would benefit least, from the revaluation of existing stocks. The USSR would undoubtedly be the major beneficiary in this respect after the United States. It would, moreover, be the largest beneficiary by far, together with South Africa, of the consequent rise in the dollar value of current gold production.[4]

These considerations explain and justify the adamant objections of the United States to a deliberate increase of gold prices in terms of the U.S. dollar. Such a decision could only be forced upon the American authorities as the outcome of a prolonged or acute economic or financial crisis, which could hardly fail to involve serious setbacks in the recent progress toward monetary convertibility and trade liberalization.

Last, but not least, the world liquidity requirements can certainly

3. See particularly Table 8, p. 49.
4. USSR gold holdings are estimated at possibly $7 billion or more, and USSR gold production in 1957 at about $600 million, nearly equal to that of South Africa, and four times as large as that of the next largest gold producing country, Canada. See Oscar L. Altman, "A Note on Gold Production and Additions to International Gold Reserves," IMF *Staff Papers*, April 1958, p. 282.

be put to better use than the financing of more and more earth-digging in South Africa, the USSR, Canada, the United States and Australia.

Flexible Exchange Rates

The most radical versions of the flexible exchange rates proposal would neatly do away with any need for international monetary reserves altogether. The foreign exchange market should be left fully to the free interplay of supply and demand, without any intervention whatsoever by Central Banks or official Stabilization Funds.

The major argument advanced in favour of this proposal is that exchange rate fluctuations would then automatically offset the impact of disparate national policies upon the internatioanl pattern of prices and costs, and preserve in this manner long-run balance in each country's international transactions without recourse to trade or exchange restrictions, and without any interference with each country's freedom to pursue whatever internal monetary and credit policies it chooses. Temporary disequilibria in the balance of payments would be recognized as such by private speculators whose purchases or sales would cushion such imbalance with only moderate movements in actual exchange rates. Persistent disequilibria would, on the other hand, elicit similarly disequilibrating speculation which would amplify the overall market imbalance, accelerate the movement of exchange rates, alert public opinion, and force the monetary authorities to readjust their policies earlier than they would have done otherwise.

A full discussion of these views would require far more space than can be given to them here. My basic objection to them, how-ever, is that actual disequilibria in the exchange markets are not exclusively related to disturbances in the international cost and price pattern. Under convertibility conditions, an excessive rate of credit expansion, particularly in a small country, may spill out very quickly into balance of payments deficits, long in advance of any substantial price increases, these being held down anyway by the competition of imports from abroad.[5] The depreciation of the

5. See my paper on "Adjusting Features in the Mechanism of the Balance of Payments and Exchange Rates," in the *Hearings before the Subcommittee on Foreign Economic Policy*, 79th Congress, Washington, D.C., 1955, pp. 134–142. An analysis of the statistical evidence assembled in a forthcoming OEEC volume on *Sources and Uses of Finance, 1948-1958* (to be published in the spring of 1960) shows that the major short term fluctuations in most European countries' balances of payments since the

national currency under the free interplay of market supply and demand would, however, stimulate increases in import prices which would, in turn, affect internal price, cost and wage levels in general. Speculation would accelerate and amplify these disequilibrating movements without, of and by itself, correcting the internal financial policies which lie at the root of the balance of payments deficits. If, however, such policies were continued indefinitely, the accelerated currency depreciation and price rises could hardly fail either to end in a currency collapse, or, more probably, to induce the authorities to resort to stringent trade and exchange restrictions, bringing to an end the flexible exchange rates experiment. If, on the other hand, the authorities decide, instead, to arrest their inflationary rates of monetary and credit expansion, price and wage rigidities will make it difficult to reverse the intervening cost increases. The new "equilibrium" exchange rates, even in the absence of renewed inflationary forces, will be lower than would have been the case if exchange flexibility and speculation had not previously driven exchange rates, import prices, and overall wage and cost levels further than they would have gone under a system of pegged exchange rates. Resistance to downward cost and wage adjustments would tend to impart a "devaluation bias" to any system of exchange rate flexibility, and this bias could not fail to make private exchange speculation far less "stabilizing" than envisaged by the proponents of exchange rate flexibility.

The theoretical expectations and probabilities briefly summarized above would seem to fit reasonably well the historical record of exchange rate flexibility, as applied by countries which did not maintain an appropriate balance in their internal monetary and credit policies. A large number of European countries did, indeed, adopt exactly the proposed system of exchange rate flexibility after the first world war, their Central Banks abstaining fully or largely from any intervention on the exchange market. In most of these cases, the ultimate result was either a complete currency collapse —as in Germany and Central Europe—or a driving down of exchange rates to levels which considerably undervalued the currency in question—as in France and Belgium. The reversal of speculative

---

war are closely related to disparate national rates of financial and monetary expansion, while prices and production tend to move in unison, under the impact of cyclical influences pervading the already closely integrated area formed by Western Europe as a whole.

transactions, following internal financial stabilization, did of course, result in large repatriation of capital and a steep recovery of the national currency on the exchange markets. This appreciation was usually stopped in fact by the authorities at a point which left the currency somewhat undervalued. When allowed, or encouraged, by the authorities to proceed further, it led to an overvalued rate which, when stabilized by official interventions, entailed heavy deflationary pressures on the economy—as in Italy and the United Kingdom. There is certainly no empirical support for the view that the wide exchange fluctuations and speculation of the 1920's helped restore anywhere equilibrium exchange rates, either while the experiment was pursued, or when it was finally terminated by *de facto* or *de jure* currency stabilization.

Some of the proponents of flexible exchange rates would concede that much and agree that such policies can only be successful if used in combination with "correct" monetary, fiscal and credit policies. In this case, however, flexible exchange rates would be likely to remain fairly stable anyway, as private speculation could then more reasonably be expected to cushion temporary disequilibria. There is no reason to think, however, that this job would be done better by private speculators than by the country's monetary authorities. The latter are presumably better informed than the first. They are also entrusted with national responsibility for the country's currency, and could hardly afford to wash their hands of any responsibility for exchange rate stabilization or management, in the hope that the job will be performed better by private speculators whose motivation may not coincide in all cases with the national interest.

The most efficient way of eliciting "stabilizing" interventions from the private capital market would indeed be for the exchange authorities to intervene systematically in the market in such a way as to keep exchange rate fluctuations within a well-known range. As long as confidence is maintained in their ability to do so, private speculators may be counted upon to buy or sell the national currency against foreign exchange whenever the limits of this range are approached. Wide rate fluctuations are not necessary to stimulate such behaviour on their part, and might on the contrary induce "destabilizing" interventions as more and more people might then be tempted to "ride the market" whenever a rising or declining trend gathers momentum.

There is, moreover, an important difference between the internal monetary impact of private stabilizing interventions, on the one hand, and of similar interventions by the Central Bank, on the other. In the latter case, the sale or purchase of foreign currencies by the Bank directly affects internal liquidity in a way which contributes to the balance of payments readjustments. The substitution of private capital movements in this role tends, on the contrary, to cushion the domestic as well as the foreign impact of the imbalance in the country's other external transactions, and to suppress at its roots the operation of the classical theory of monetary adjustment. Such "sterilization" or "neutralization" of the domestic impact of external imbalance may be desirable in some cases, but not in all. The Central Bank is always free, of course, whenever it deems it desirable, to offset by deliberate policy action, the automatic bias toward "neutralization" implicit in private stabilizing speculation. Such "neutralization" of "neutralization," however, complicates rather than simplifies the job of monetary management. On balance, stabilizing interventions by the Central Bank itself, with their implicit bias toward internal monetary adjustments, would often present advantages over private stabilizing interventions with their implicit bias toward neutralization.

There remains, however, a hard core of validity in the theory of flexible exchange rates. This is that exchange rate readjustment to "realistic" levels is preferable to vain and costly attempts to preserve "unrealistic" exchange levels through persistent reserve losses, foreign borrowings, or trade and exchange restrictions. All three of these techniques, and particularly the first two, may be desirable to defend an equilibrated rate of exchange against the impact of purely temporary imbalance. The third of them, however—*i.e.* trade and exchange restrictions—, has often been used for prolonged periods in the face of fundamental price and cost maladjustments. The damage to the national economy is then obvious. Temporary restrictions, widely recognized as such, may induce a postponement of expenditures until the restrictions are lifted. Long lasting restrictions are most unlikely to have such an effect. They will induce instead a drying up of capital imports, an expansion of legal—or illegal—capital exports, and a reshuffling of expenditures from prohibited imports to domestically produced goods. If substantial unemployment prevails at the time, this latter effect may be desirable, but still less so than an exchange rate readjustment which would stimulate exports as well as reduce imports, restore balance in the capital market and avoid unnecessary distortions in resource allocation. If, however, as is frequently the case, the deficit coincides with a situation of full or overfull, employment, the diversion of demand from foreign to domestic sources of supply can only lead to a corresponding reduction in the country's exporting capacity, and/or an accentuation of internal inflationary pressures.

A readjustment of exchange rates would be preferable in both cases to a permanent system of trade or exchange restrictions.[6] After a period of disturbance, or pending the full success of an internal stabilization program, it may also be advisable for the monetary authorities to postpone temporarily any commitment to a new and stable exchange rate whose "correct" level may be difficult to gauge under the circumstances.[7]

These solid arguments against abusive, and largely illusory, resort to restrictions and against the obstinate maintenance of exchange rates at unrealistic levels should not be extrapolated into a blanket approval of flexible rates as a universal panacea for balance of payments management. Neither do they offer a satisfactory solution to the international liquidity problem raised in Part One of this book. Adequate reserve levels are no substitute for desirable exchange readjustments, but inadequate reserve levels will still entail undesirable recourse to exchange devaluation or restrictions, and introduce in international trade and payments unnecessary disturbances highly dangerous for the smooth functioning and effective preservation of currency convertibility.

6. In the second, overfull employment case, however, a downward readjustment of overall expenditures to a level corresponding to the maximum practicable use of the country's productive resources will certainly be necessary. and may even in some cases obviate the need for any exchange rate readjustment. See the article quoted above in footnote 5, pp. 82-83.

7. For a (strongly qualified) defense of the exchange rates policies pursued by the International Monetary Fund, see my *Europe and the Money Muddle*, pp. 116–124.

CHAPTER 2

The Internationalization
of Foreign Exchange
Reserves

Gold has long ceased to provide adequate amounts of international liquidity for an expanding world economy. New gold production and USSR sales supplied considerably less than one half of the increase in world reserves over the years 1950–1957, and are unlikely to cover much more than one third to one half of prospective reserve requirements in the foreseeable future.[1]

Barring a drastic revaluation of gold prices, the maintenance of adequate reserve levels will thus continue to depend on the growth of foreign exchange reserves as a supplement to gold itself. This, however, cannot fail to increase further and further the vulnerability of the world monetary system to shifts of confidence—justified or unjustified—in the national currencies actually used as reserve media. A repetition of 1931 would, at some point, become well-nigh unavoidable.

The logical solution of this dilemma would lie in the "internationalization" of the foreign exchange component of monetary reserves. The use of *national* currencies as *international* reserves constitutes indeed a "built-in de-stabilizer" in the world monetary system. The free choice of reserve holders will normally tend to concentrate on the "safest" currencies available for this purpose, *i.e.* on the currencies of the major creditor countries. In accumulating such currencies as reserves, however, reserve holders are really extending "unrequited" loans to these countries, and increasing further the natural hardness of their currencies. Such lending, moreover, does not relieve the international liquidity shortage if the key currency

1. See above, Part One, Ch. 5, esp. Tables 8, 11, and 14.

countries increase their own gold holdings *pari passu* with the rise in their international short-term liabilities. They can relieve the situation, and avoid a "scarce key currency" condition from developing, only if they succeed in re-lending abroad—or giving away in the form of grants—amounts sufficient to finance not only their current account surpluses, but also the inflow of unrequited borrowings corresponding to the accumulation of their currency as reserves by other countries. If this is done, and as long as it continues to be done, the international liquidity problem will be solved, and the authorities of the key currency countries may possibly welcome the political influence which can be derived from this increase in their international lending capacity.[2]

The process, however, is bound to come to an end at some point. The key currency countries cannot afford to let their net reserve position deteriorate indefinitely. If they did, their currency would stop, in any case, to be considered as the safest, and the time would come when other countries would cease accumulating it, and might even begin converting some of their outstanding holdings into gold or other currencies. When this stage is reached, the key currency country will be faced with difficult readjustments in the previously built-in structure of its international transactions. Isolationist, economy-minded, and protectionist groups will find in such a situation powerful arguments in favor of a curtailment of foreign aid programs and of a reversal in the liberal trading policies previously pursued. These types of remedies, however, may be not only internationally damaging, but also less effective in practice than would appear at first, since the curtailment of both foreign aid and imports is most likely to be offset, to a substantial extent, by a decline in exports.

Whatever the policies adopted to readjust the country's balance of payments and arrest the gold outflow, their success will inevitably entail, at the very least, a cessation of the key currency country's current contributions to the solution of the international liquidity problem. Their failure, on the other hand, may have far worse consequences still by stimulating large-scale liquidation of outstanding foreign held balances, and triggering an international finan-

2. Economic advantages may also flow from the fact that the loans extended by the key currency countries will usually bear higher rates of interest than those paid on their short-term liabilities and may help promote exports to the borrowing countries. The first of these two considerations, however, obviously does not apply to the re-export of capital in the form of grants.

cial panic involving other currencies as well. This is precisely what happened in 1931, and led temporarily to the near-elimination of foreign exchange balances from monetary reserves by all countries outside the sterling area. Nobody can deny the role of these events in the intensification of the world crisis in the early 1930's.

In brief, the constitution of international reserves in the form of a national currency tends to stimulate unrequited lending to the major creditor country and add to the difficulties which it may already face in financing its surpluses abroad. If it fails in this task, the gold shortage will remain unsolved but appear instead in the guise of a shortage of the main creditor country's currency. If, on the other hand, it redistributes abroad sufficient grants and credits to finance not only its current account surpluses, but to offset in addition the unrequited inflow of short-term funds from abroad, its net reserve position will gradually deteriorate to the point where its currency no longer appears as absolutely safe to reserve holders. The flow of reserve funds will then tend to slow down, or even to reverse itself, in such a way as to accentuate again overall balance of payments disequilibria, rather than cushion them. The readjustments imposed at this stage upon the creditor country will, if successfully carried out, arrest at the very least its previous contribution to the maintenance of an adequate level of international liquidity. There is a serious danger, however, that a less skillful handling of the situation may result in a sharp reversal of liberal trading policies throughout the world, or even trigger large scale movements of short-term funds from one currency into another and from all currencies into gold.

The most logical escape from these difficulties is obvious enough, and would have been adopted long ago if it were not for the enormous difficulties involved in overcoming the forces of inertia and in reaching agreement among several scores of countries on the multiple facets of a rational system of international money and credit creation. This is, of course, the only explanation for the survival of gold itself as the ultimate means of international monetary settlements. Nobody could ever have conceived of a more absurd waste of human resources than to dig gold in distant corners of the earth for the sole purpose of transporting it and re-burying it immediately afterwards in other deep holes, especially excavated to receive it and heavily guarded to protect it. The history of human institutions, however, has a logic of its own. Gold as a commodity enjoyed undoubted advantages over other commodities that could alternatively be used as money. The substitution of debt or paper money for commodity money within each country's national borders was a slow, gradual, and still recent phenomenon in world affairs. Its extension to the international sphere is even more recent and has also developed haphazardly under the pressure of circumstances rather than as a rational act of creation on the part of any national or international authority. This explains the present, and totally irrational, use of *national* currencies as *international* reserves. Yet, the proliferation of regional, international, and supranational agencies since the war is slowly laying the groundwork for further, and long overdue, adaptations in the international monetary system, and particularly for the internationalization of the fiduciary portion— foreign exchange—of countries' monetary reserves.

This was indeed the keystone of the famous Keynes Plan for an International Clearing Union.[3] The one vital provision of the plan, on which its whole structure rested, lay in the proposed commitment of all member states to accept, in lieu of gold payment and without any limit whatsoever, bancor transfers to their credit in the books of the Union in full settlement of any balances due to them from any other members (Article 6, paragraph 6). Of and by itself, such a provision would have endowed the Clearing Union with an equally *unlimited* lending capacity, since "no member State would be entitled to demand gold from the Clearing Union against its balance of bancor." This was made explicit in Article 29 and also in Article 5: "If no credits can be removed outside the clearing system, but only transferred within it, the Union can never be in any difficulty as regards the honoring of checks drawn upon it. It can make what advances it wishes to any of its members with the assurance that the proceeds can only be transferred to the clearing account of another member. Its sole task is to see to it that its members keep the rules and that the advances made to each of them are prudent and advisable for the Union as a whole."

Keynes correctly characterized this vital feature of the Plan as the logical extension into the international field of the essential

3. All the following references will be to the official text of these "Proposals by British Experts for an International Clearing Union," dated April 8, 1943, as reproduced in the *Proceedings and Documents of the United Nations Monetary and Financial Conference*, U.S. Government Printing Office, Washington, 1948, Vol. II, pp. 1548–1573. For a fuller discussion and criticism of the Keynes Plan, see *Europe and the Money Muddle*, pp. 93–109.

principle underlying the development of national banking systems. Keynes' remarks on this point are well worth re-reading, and deserve the extensive quotations which follow.

The acceptance of unlimited bancor accounts by creditor countries would be no real burden to them. "For the accumulation of a credit balance with the Clearing Union would resemble the importation of gold in signifying that the country holding it is abstaining voluntarily from the immediate use of purchasing power. But it would not involve, as would the importation of gold, the withdrawal of this purchasing power from circulation or the exercise of a deflationary and contractionist pressure on the whole world, including in the end the creditor country itself. Under the proposed plan, therefore, no country suffers injury (but on the contrary) by the fact that the command over resources, which it does not itself choose to employ for the time being, is not withdrawn from use. The accumulation of bancor credit does not curtail in the least its capacity or inducement either to produce or to consume" (Article 11).

"In short, the analogy with a national banking system is complete. No depositor in a local bank suffers because the balances, which he leaves idle, are employed to finance the business of someone else. Just as the development of national banking systems served to offset a deflationary pressure which would have prevented otherwise the development of modern industry, so by extending the same principle into the international field we may hope to offset the contractionist pressure which might otherwise overwhelm in social disorder and disappointment the good hopes of our modern world. The substitution of a credit mechanism in place of hoarding would have repeated in the international field the same miracle, already performed in the domestic field, of turning a stone into bread" (Article 12).

"No particular member States have to engage their own resources as such to the support of other particular States or of any of the international projects or policies adopted. They have only to agree in general that, if they find themselves with surplus resources which for the time being they do not themselves wish to employ, these resources may go into the general pool and be put to work on approved purposes. This costs the surplus country nothing because it is not asked to part permanently, or even for any specified period, with such resources, which it remains free to expend and employ for its own purposes whenever it chooses; in which case the burden of

finance is passed on to the next recipient, again for only so long as
the recipient has no use for the money. As pointed out above, this
merely amounts to extending to the international sphere the methods
of any domestic banking system, which are in the same sense 'impersonal' inasmuch as there is no call on the particular depositor
either to support as such the purposes for which his banker makes
advances or to forego permanently the use of his deposit. There is
no countervailing objection except that which applies equally to the
technique of domestic banking, namely that it is capable of the abuse
of creating excessive purchasing power and hence an inflation of
prices. In our efforts to avoid the opposite evil, we must not lose sight
of this risk . . . But it is no more reason for refusing the advantages
of international banking than the similar risk in the domestic field
is a reason to return to the practices of the seventeenth century gold-
smiths (which are what we are still following in the international
field) and to forego the vast expansion of production which banking
principles have made possible. Where financial contributions are
required for some purpose of general advantage it is a great facility
not to have to ask for specific contributions from any named country,
but to depend rather on the anonymous and impersonal aid of the
system as a whole. We have here a genuine organ of truly international government" (Article 40).

The last words of this quotation reflect the only valid objection
to the whole argumentation of Keynes. The objection is political,
not economic, in nature. From a narrowly economic point of view,
Keynes is perfectly correct. Bancor accounts would, under his plan,
have been just as good as gold. Although the bancor accumulation
of creditor countries would serve as a basis for the extension of
credit to others, the liquidity of the creditors' accounts would remain
unimpaired, since they could always be used as freely as gold itself
to make payments anywhere in the world. The political objection,
however, was a double one.

First and foremost is the risk, admitted by Keynes, of an unwise
use of the Clearing Union's lending facilities to finance inflationary,
rather than merely expansionist, policies throughout the world. This
would reduce the real value of the creditors' accounts—including
their gold as well as their bancor reserves—and expose them to
stronger inflationary pressures than would have been the case in
the absence of such inflationary lending by the Union. This would
appear, on the surface, as a reasonable *economic* objection to the

Plan. If, however, the creditor countries themselves were in agreement with the Union's lending policies, they could hardly complain about the consequences of decisions in which they fully concurred. The core of the problem lies therefore in the voting procedures of the Union, and in the loss of sovereignty which they may involve. Various safeguards might conceivably be set up and allay the creditors' legitimate fears in this respect. Those provided in the Keynes Plan, however, were totally inadequate, and little ingenuity was shown by any of its negotiators in devising better ones.[4]

A second objection, from the point of view of prospective creditor countries, lay in the "impersonality" or "anonymity" of the Union's lending. Keynes saw in this a major virtue of the Plan, as it was indeed from an international viewpoint and, even more, from the point of view of prospective borrowers such as the United Kingdom in the early postwar years. It would also entail, however, a diminution of the political influence and bargaining power that the lending nations could otherwise derive from direct loan negotiations with the borrowing countries. Properly speaking, this should not be regarded as a legitimate objection to the Plan, but rather as an obstacle in the way of its successful negotiation in a nationalistic world.

The predominantly political nature of these difficulties must be fully recognized in trying to devise realistic formulas for feasible progress toward international agreement in this field. One of the major implications of such an approach will lie in distinguishing what may be accomplished through world-wide agreements and what may prove achievable only on the regional scale within smaller and more homogeneous groups of highly interdependent countries, keenly conscious of their interdependence, and better prepared by a common geographical and historical background to understand one another's problems and policies.

4. A simple, but extreme, solution, could have been to impose the unanimity rule on all important lending decisions of the Union. That this might not have been as paralyzing a provision as might appear at first can be demonstrated by the experience of OEEC, in which this rule has always been observed. Less extreme solutions will be discussed later in this book.

CHAPTER 3

The International Monetary Fund Today

The International Monetary Fund, as presently constituted, can only bring a limited, although still extremely valuable, contribution to the world liquidity problem.

Past and Current Loans

The Fund's lending operations, over its twelve years of existence, are summarized in Table 15. Gross loans totalled $759 million in the first three years (1947–1949) but were largely repaid in the following six years, bringing down the amount of outstanding loans to only $234 million at the end of 1955. The Suez crisis was followed by an unprecedented level of activity. The Fund's net lending rose by nearly $1,500 million in two years and has remained since then at a cumulative level of approximately $1,700 million.

There are also outstanding, in addition, about $900 million of unused drawing rights under so-called stand-by agreements, and all countries have been assured "the overwhelming benefit of the doubt" for borrowings within their so-called "gold tranche," *i.e.* up to the amounts actually contributed by them to the Fund in the form of paid-in gold subscriptions and of the Fund's use of their national currency subscriptions. Taken together, these unused facilities amount to about $2,450 million for the major creditor countries listed in Table 15, $740 million for the United Kingdom, and $300 million for all other countries taken together.[5]

5. The outstanding Fund loans ($1,700 million at the end of 1958) are included as part of the borrowing countries' gross reserves in all the tables presented in this book. Net claims on the Fund and drawing rights available under stand-by agreements are not reported, however, as part of the countries' monetary reserves.

TABLE 15

IMF Loans and Lending Commitments
(*in millions of U.S. dollars*)

A. IMF Lending, 1947-1958						
	Apparent Borrowings (1)	Repurchases of Borrowers' Currencies by Other Members (2)	True Borrowings (3 = 1 − 2)	Repayments by Borrowers (4)	Net Borrowings (5 = 3 − 4)	Cumulative Net Borrowings at end of period (6)
I. *1947-1949*	*777*	*17*	*759*	*2*	*757*	*757*
1947	468	6	462	—	462	462
1948	208	11	197	—	197	658
1949	101	—	101	2	99	757
II. *1950-1955*	*439*	*186*	*254*	*777*	*− 523*	*234*
1950	—	—	—	24	− 24	733
1951	35	28	7	46	− 39	694
1952	85	—	85	102	− 16	678
1953	230	158	72	163	− 91	587
1954	62	—	62	210	− 148	439
1955	28	—	28	232	− 205	234
III. *1956-1957*	*1,670*	—	*1,670*	*177*	*1,493*	*1,727*
1956	693	—	693	113	579	814
1957	977	—	977	64	913	1,727
IV. *1958*	*338*	*21*	*317*	*348*	*− 31*	*1,696*
V. *Total* . . .	**3,224**	**224**	**3,000**	**1,304**	**1,696**	

B. IMF Unused Lending Commitments, at the End of 1958	
I. *Undrawn Amounts Under Stand-by Arrangements*	**911**
A. United Kingdom	*737*
B. Other Countries	*183*
II. *Net Credits and Gold-Tranche Commitments*, of which:	**2,580**
A. Major Creditor Countries	*2,452*
1. United States	1,958
2. Germany	147
3. Canada	90
4. Netherlands	69
5. Japan	62
6. Belgium	56
7. Italy	45
8. Sweden	25
B. Other Countries[1]	*128*

Footnote: 1. After elimination of $5 million overlap with stand-by arrangements.

TABLE 16
IMF Currency and Gold Transactions, 1947-19
(*in millions of U.S. dollars*)

Fund's Receipts (+) or Disbursements (−)	U.S. Dollars	German Marks	Canadian Dollars	Belgian Francs
1. Member's Borrowings (+)	—	—	—	+83
2. Other Members' Borrowings (−) . .	−2,916	−69	−15	−11
3. Total Net Borrowings (1+2) . . .	*−2,916*	*−69*	*−15*	*+72*
4. Repayments	+1,000	—	—	−72
5. Cumulative Net Borrowings (3+4) .	*−1,916*	*−69*	*−15*	—
6. Other[1]	−46	—	—	—
7. Total Fund's Receipts or Disbursements (5 + 6)	−1,962	−69	−15	—
8. Purchases of Currency against Gold[2] .	+692	—	—	—
9. Total Change in Fund's Holdings (7+8)	*−1,270*	*−69*	*−15*	—
10. Residual Holdings[3] (11+9) . . .	792	183	210	169
11. Quota Subscription[3]	2,062	252	225	169

Footnotes: 1. Fund's administrative expenditures (−), and miscellaneous receipts (+) arising mos from payment of charges in the paying member's currency.

2. Including $92 million directly received from members in U.S. dollars in lieu of gold subscriptions.

3. Excluding all unpaid subscriptions.

4. Including $2 million due to be paid in instalments by withdrawing member (Czechoslovakia) by J 1961.

Lending Capacity

The future lending capacity of the Fund—and thus its ability to alleviate the prospective world liquidity shortage—is far more difficult to appraise.

The sum of all quotas measures both the total lending commitments and borrowing "facilities" of the Fund's members. Since, however, the same country cannot be at the same time a net lender and a net borrower, the maximum net lending commitments usable at any time cannot possibly exceed half of this sum, unless widespread waivers allowed debtor countries to borrow in excess of their total quotas. The extreme limit of the Fund's present lending capacity could be estimated, on this basis, at about $4.3 billion.[6] This would be raised to about $6.75 billion after the quota increases

6. Members' quotas totalled about $9.2 billion at the end of 1958, but included nearly $950 millions of unpaid subscriptions. Unless otherwise noted, all the estimates discussed in this paper assume full payment of these subscriptions, with the exception of that of Nationalist China whose large unpaid quota ($550 million) obviously bears no relationship to its prospective lending to, or borrowing from, the Fund.

Dutch Guilders	Pounds Sterling	Other Currencies	All Currencies	Gold	Total
+144	+862	+2,135	+3,224[4]	x	+3,224
−5	−208	—	−3,224[4]	x	−3,224
+139	+654	+2,135	x	x	x
−39	−108	−985	−305	+305	x
—	+545	+1,150	−305[5]	+305[5]	x
—	+13	+4	−29	+52	+22
—	+558	+1,154	−334	+356	+22
—	—	—	+692	−692	x
—	+558	+1,154	+358	−335	+22
206	1,618	3,562	6,740[4]	1,532[6]	8,272
206	1,060	2,408	6,382	1,867	8,249

5. Represents the difference, received in gold by the Fund, between the currencies "sold to the Fund" net borrowers ($1,696 million) and the currencies of creditor countries "sold by the Fund" in the course these operations ($2,000 million).

6. Including $200 million in U.S. Treasury Bills and funds awaiting investment obtained from proceeds gold sales and reconvertible into the same quantity of gold upon termination of investment.

recently approved by the Fund's Board of Governors have gone into effect.

This, however, is a rather theoretical estimate. It should first be modified to take account of past Fund operations which have deeply modified the outstanding lending commitments and borrowing rights of a number of countries. These operations are summarized in Table 16. The Fund's resources as of the end of 1958—excluding all unpaid subscriptions—can be read from line 10 of this Table. They included $1.5 billion of gold and $6.7 billion in about three scores of members' currencies. More than half of this latter sum, however, was made up of currencies for which the Fund has never received any request, and which are most unlikely ever to be sold by it in any significant amounts. Most of them are indeed currencies of underdeveloped countries—such as India, Brazil, Pakistan, etc.— who should be expected to be frequent borrowers from the Fund, rather than net lenders to it. The Fund's holdings of the six currencies ever lent by it in its twelve years of operation totalled little more than $3 billion, of which more than $1.6 billion, however, was in the currency of the Fund's largest net borrower, and less than $1.2

billion in the only three currencies ever *really* borrowed from the Fund on a net basis.[7]

A more realistic, even though still highly conjectural, appraisal of the Fund's true lending capacity may be gauged from Table 17. Ten alternative calculations are presented, based upon different assumptions as to the currencies requested from the Fund by future borrowers. For simplicity's sake, only eight currencies have been retained for this purpose, and some of them have been grouped together rather arbitrarily. It will generally be agreed that very few of the other Fund currencies could be added to this list. This would not, in any case, increase substantially the resulting estimates of the Fund's lending capacity, as the amounts involved would be small at best, and could not possibly be used simultaneously with the eight currencies shown without widespread and large scale waivers of quota limits on the remaining borrowing countries.

If the U.S. dollar remains in strong demand by the Fund's borrowers (lines VI 1, a, b, and c), the Fund's maximum lending capacity, after the increase in quotas, would be of the order of $4.5 to $7.4 billion, depending on how many—and how much—of the other currencies are also in demand. The latter sum, however, could not actually be lent by the Fund without substantial waivers (more than $1.5 billion) of quota limits on all other members' borrowings.

The substitution of sterling for the dollar as the main currency in strong demand (lines VI 2, a, b, and c) would not modify greatly the above estimates, except that the substitution of the United States for the United Kingdom as an extreme borrower would enable the same lending capacity—and indeed much more—to be used even in the absence of any waivers of the borrowing quotas.

In the absence of any demand for either U.S. dollars or pounds sterling (line VI 3), the Fund's maximum lending capacity would remain well below $6 billion.

Finally, if both U.S. dollars and pounds sterling were in strong demand (lines VI 4, a, b, and c), the Fund's lending capacity could be of the order of $6.7 billion to $9.5 billion, any amounts in excess of $7.5 billion, however, requiring once more extensive waivers in favor of borrowers.

All these are, of course, extreme hypotheses, which suggest the

7. The occasional Fund's sales of sterling, Dutch guilders and Belgian francs have always been offset, or indeed far more than offset, by previous borrowings of these three countries from the Fund. See lines 1, 2, and 3 of Table 16.

TABLE 17

IMF Lending Capacity

(*in millions of U.S. dollars*)

	Fund's Lending Capacity			Quota Borrowing Facilities of Other Members					
	Current Fund Holdings	Proposed Quota Increases	Total	Total	U.S.	U.K.	Other Drawn Currencies (IV)	Other Major Currencies (V)	Other Countries
I. Gold	1,532	1,210	**2,742**						
II. U.S. Dollars . . .	792	1,031	**1.823**						
III. Pounds Sterling . .	1,618	487	**2,106**						
IV. Other Currencies Drawn in Past Operations .	768	718	**1,486**						
1. German Marks . .	183	343	**526**						
2. Canadian Dollars . .	210	187	**397**						
3. Dutch Guilders . .	206	103	**309**						
4. Belgian Francs . .	169	84	**253**						
V. Other Major Currencies	975	384	**1,359**						
1. French Francs . .	787	197	**984**						
2. Japanese Yens . .	187	187	**375**						
VI. *Alternative Patterns of Lending Capacity:*									
1. *Gold and U.S. Dollars*									
a. only (I+II) . .	2,324	2,241	**4,565**	9,774	—	1,794	2,688	1,215	4,077
b. plus other drawn currencies (I+II+IV)	3,092	2,959	**6,051**	7,086	—	1,794	—	1,215	4,077
c. plus other major currencies (I+II+IV+V) . . .	4,067	3,343	**7,410**	5,871	—	1,794	—	—	4,077
2. *Gold and Pounds Sterling*									
a. only (I+III) .	3,150	1,697	**4,847**	14,407	6,427	—	2,688	1,215	4,077
b. plus other drawn currencies (I+III+IV)	3,918	2,415	**6,333**	11,719	6,427	—	—	1,215	4,077
c. plus other major currencies (I+III+IV+V) . .	4,893	2,799	**7,692**	10,504	6,427	—	—	—	4,077
3. *Gold and All Currencies Listed except U.S. Dollars and Pounds Sterling* (I+IV+V) .	3,275	2,312	**5,587**	8,221	6,427	1,794	—	—	—
4. *Gold, U.S. Dollars and Pounds Sterling*									
a. only (I+II+III)	3,942	2,728	**6,671**	7,980	—	—	2,688	1,215	4,077
b. plus other drawn currencies (I+II+III+IV) . . .	4,710	3,446	**8,157**	5,292	—	—	—	1,215	4,077
c. plus other major currencies (I+II+III+IV+V) .	5,685	3,830	**9,516**	4,077	—	—	—	—	4,077

159796

maximum limits rather than the plausible scope of the Fund's future lending. Loans much in excess of, let us say, $5 billion could hardly fail to be accompanied with a threatening scarcity of some creditors' currencies and would probably require a depletion of the Fund's gold assets endangering its ability to honor, in the desired currencies, its moral commitment to give every member the "overwhelming benefit of the doubt" to drawings within its gold tranche.

Yet, even a $5 billion lending capacity should be more than adequate to meet for several years to come the world liquidity shortage, roughly estimated at some $5 billion to $15 billion over the next decade.[8] This is all the more true as the reserve position of all major reserve holders, outside the United States, improved considerably during 1958. These countries—including the United Kingdom and France—are less likely to require any large scale Fund assistance in the near future. The Fund will thus be able to devote most of its resources to loans to the non-industrialized countries whose need for such assistance is greatest, particularly in view of the alarming deterioration of their balance of payments and reserve position during the last few years.

The breathing space thus made available by the increases in the Fund's quotas should be used by governments and their technical experts to explore the bolder and more imaginative reforms called for to adjust international monetary institutions to present-day needs and possibilities.

The most fundamental deficiency of the present system, and the main danger to its future stability, lies in the fact that it leaves the satisfactory development of world monetary liquidity primarily dependent upon an admittedly insufficient supply of new gold and an admittedly dangerous and haphazard expansion in the short-term indebtedness of the key currency countries. The most logical solution to the problem would lie in the substitution of IMF balances for

8. These figures, however, are not really comparable. First of all, borrowings within the gold tranche are included in this $5 billion estimate and would constitute merely a recovery by the borrowers of amounts they have themselves lent to the Fund. Some of the lending countries, moreover, do not regard as monetary reserves their net claims on the Fund arising from their gold contribution and the use of their national currency subscription. The main contribution of IMF lending to world liquidity, therefore, lies much less in the creation of additional liquidity than in the "activation" of the pre-existing stock of world reserves. The "inactive" reserves of creditor countries are placed at the disposal of, and used by, borrowing countries whose reserve levels are particularly deficient. To this extent, the Fund's loans increase the velocity, rather than the quantity, of world reserves.

such national currencies in all member countries' monetary reserves.

The acceptance of such a solution—under the necessary guarantees outlined below—would also eliminate most of the unnecessary complexities and limitations in the Fund's borrowing and lending techniques which now arise from their dependence upon fixed subscriptions of national currencies. The Fund's lending capacity could then be derived instead from the normal accumulation by members of a portion of their monetary reserves in the form of IMF balances, as fully and internationally usable as gold itself. As contrasted with present quota subscriptions, such balances would involve no sacrifice of liquidity for their holders, and their amounts could be made to adjust in a flexible manner to the future evolution of each member's reserve position. This would avoid the need to renegotiate periodically with several scores of countries quota increases, a large portion of which merely serves to flood the Fund's coffers with millions, and even billions, of afghanis, pesos, cruzeiros, yuans, dinars, bolivianos, etc. which are most unlikely ever to be of any use to the institution.

The essential feature of such a solution is, of course, identical to the bancor proposal of Keynes discussed on pp. 89–93 above. The concrete proposals that follow, however, differ in nearly all other respects from the Keynes plan and these differences are, in turn, dictated by two major preoccupations. The first is to meet squarely the political and economic arguments raised against it and which made it unnegotiable in practice, particularly from the point of view of the prospective creditor countries. The second is to remove a number of weaknesses of Keynes' proposals, ascribable in most cases to peculiarly British concerns and interests and to the highly abnormal and difficult conditions rightly expected by him to arise in the early postwar years.

CHAPTER 4

A New Charter for the
International Monetary Fund

The keystone of our proposals would be the substitution of IMF balances for balances in national currencies—*i.e.* mostly dollars and sterling—in all member countries' monetary reserves. Such balances should be made equivalent in all respects to gold itself and as widely usable and acceptable in world payments.

The latter purpose would have been achieved in the Keynes plan through a binding obligation on each member country to accept unlimited amounts of bancor in settlement of any claims accumulated by it on any other member country. The bancor accounts thus credited to it could be spent freely for similar settlements to others, but would not give it any right whatsoever to withdraw gold from the Clearing Union. The acceptance of such a proposal would have endowed the Union with an equally unlimited lending capacity, restrained only in practice by the insufficient limitations placed by other provisions of the plan on each member's borrowing right or quota.

The major objection raised against the Keynes plan lay precisely in the enormous inflationary pressures to which the prospective surplus countries would expose themselves by accepting such wide commitments to bancor accumulation. A second objection lay in the fact that the creation of bancor money by the Union would not displace, but add to, the expansionary influence associated with any further growth of sterling and dollar balances. The maintenance of dollar and sterling balances as alternative, or supplementary, means of international settlement—alongside with gold and bancor—also meant that the Keynes plan would not have removed entirely the dangers and weaknesses arising from the operation of a gold exchange standard. Finally, further objections were validly raised against the auto-

102

maticity of the large borrowing rights conferred upon future deficit countries.

These objections were met in fact by the abandonment of the key feature of the plan, and the replacement of bancor accounts by national quotas, dependent largely on national currency subscriptions to the IMF. The proposals that follow would, on the contrary, preserve the core of the Keynes plan mechanism, while meeting frontally the objections raised against it. They would retain IMF—or bancor—accounts as a fully multilateral means of settlement, thus simplifying vastly the lending and borrowing operations of the institution, and guaranteeing in a much firmer fashion the continued interconvertibility of all member currencies against a relapse into discrimination and bilateralism in world trade and payments.

Sources and Limits of the Fund's Overall Lending Capacity

The IMF lending capacity would be based, as in the Keynes plan, on the accumulation of bancor accounts—in the form of deposits with the IMF—by member countries as part and parcel of their total monetary reserves, alongside of gold itself and fully equivalent to it in international settlements. This basic objective, however, requires neither that the Fund be endowed with an *unlimited*—and potentially inflationary—lending capacity, nor that each member country commit itself in advance to accumulate *unlimited* amounts of bancor in settlement of its surpluses.

The overall lending capacity of the Fund can properly be limited to the creation of bancor amounts sufficient to preserve an adequate level of international liquidity. Various criteria could be retained for this purpose. The simplest one might be to limit the Fund's net lending, over any twelve months period, to a total amount which would, together with current increases in the world stock of monetary gold, increase total world reserves by, let us say, 3 to 5 per cent a year.[1] The exact figure could not, of course, be determined scientifically and would, in any case, depend in practice upon the compromise between divergent national viewpoints which would emerge from the negotiation of the new Fund Agreement. A reasonably conservative solution would be to retain a 3 per cent figure as definitely non-inflationary, and to require qualified votes (two thirds, three fourths,

1. See above, pp. 47–50.

and ultimately four fifths of the total voting power, or even unanimity) to authorize lending in excess of 3, 4 or 5 per cent a year.[2]

Assuming, for instance, that monetary gold stocks continue to increase by $700 million or $800 million a year, the Fund's annual lending quota based on a 3 per cent rate could be roughly estimated today at about $800 million to $900 million. A 4 per cent rate would raise this to about $1.4 billion, and 5 per cent to about $2 billion a year.[3] These estimates would rise gradually, but slowly, with further increases in world reserves. They could decrease as well as increase, on the other hand, with future fluctuations in the current additions to the world monetary gold stock.

Minimum Deposit Requirements

What provisions would be necessary to induce member countries to finance such lending by the Fund through the accumulation of an equivalent amount of Fund balances as part of the annual increase in their total monetary reserves?

Most member countries have, for many years past, held a considerable portion of their monetary reserves in the form of foreign exchange—primarily U.S. dollars and pounds sterling—rather than gold. The percentage of foreign exchange reserves to total reserves averaged at the end of 1957 some 30 per cent for the world as a whole, and as much as 55 per cent for countries other than the United States and the United Kingdom.[4] During the five years preceding the Suez crisis, official dollar balances alone increased at an average pace of nearly $1 billion a year.

The major stimuli to such accumulation are, of course, the lower costs incidental to the use of key currencies rather than gold in world settlements, and the earnings derived from the portion of a country's reserves held in the form of foreign exchange. The major deterrents to such accumulation, on the other hand, are the risks of exchange fluctuations, inconvertibility, blocking, or even default, inseparable from holdings in a foreign country's currency.

The shift from national currency balances to balances with the

2. Alternative criteria, more logical but also more difficult to define concretely, might be derived from the current trend of some international price index reflecting inflationary or deflationary pressures on the world economy.

3. These calculations are based on the IMF estimates of world reserves—excluding international institutions—of about $54 billion at the end of 1958.

4. See Tables 3 (p. 40) and 12 (p. 55).

IMF could preserve fully the same incentives and decrease considerably at the same time the weight of the deterrents mentioned above. The Fund's earnings on its own loans and investments[5] should be distributed among members *pro rata* of the balances held by them with the institution. These balances should—as all other Fund accounts—be expressed in a gold unit, and escape therefore the foreign exchange risk always attached to foreign exchange holdings in national currencies. They would similarly remain unaffected by any inconvertibility decision adopted by any individual member of the Fund. They could, at any time, be used by their holders as freely and widely as gold itself to make payments to any other member country, and even to non-members.[6] These provisions should make it possible for all countries to count their balances with the Fund as a normal and valuable component of their monetary reserves, and as fully equivalent to gold for the calculation of reserve or gold cover requirements wherever legal provisions still exist in this respect.

These various advantages should ensure a considerable demand for Fund balances on the part of most member countries, and particularly on the part of those which are already holding a large portion of their monetary reserves in the form of foreign exchange rather than gold. Members' voluntary holdings of Fund balances might well exceed after a time the amounts needed to finance the Fund's lending operations, in which case a growing portion of the Fund's assets would take the form of gold.

This is not likely to become true, however, until members have grown fully familiar with the system and with the security, liquidity, and earning power of this new form of reserve assets. In the initial years at least, it will be necessary to require Fund members to hold with the institution balances amply sufficient to finance its lending

5. See below, pp. 115–119. Since the Fund, however, would hold in non-earning gold a portion of the assets corresponding to its deposit liabilities to members, the rate of earnings on such deposits would be somewhat lower than the rates of earnings on the Fund on its loans and investments. On the other hand, the Fund might attract free deposits by paying a higher rate of interest on these than on minimum, compulsory deposits.

6. The membership of the Fund now includes practically all countries outside the Soviet bloc, except Switzerland and New Zealand. Some further efforts could be made to induce these two countries to join a reformed IMF, and the rest of our discussion will assume that these efforts have been successful. The special arrangements otherwise needed to enable members to draw on their Fund account for settlements to non-members would not create any serious financial burden for the Fund.

and to guarantee—through a sufficient accumulation of gold reserves
—the full convertibility of Fund balances into any currency, even the
"hardest," actually needed in settlements.

Both of these purposes could be achieved most simply by requiring
all members to hold in the form of Fund deposits a certain proportion
of their gross monetary reserves. All would agree to accept such
deposits in settlement of their international claims without limit,
but would have the right to convert at any time into gold, if they so
wish, deposits accrued to their Fund account in excess of this minimum requirement. This obligation would substitute for the present
system of Fund quotas, and offer considerable advantages over it from
the point of view of individual members as well as from the point of
view of the Fund itself.

The first of these advantages would lie in the fact that such balances
with the Fund would remain as fully liquid and usable in payments
as gold itself, and should therefore—as already noted above—be
considered as part of each country's monetary reserves. The maintenance of a portion of a country's reserves in this form would therefore be no burden on it and would not raise the internal financing
problems which some countries now find in financing their quota
subscription to the Fund.[7]

The second advantage is that deposit obligations would adjust
automatically to fluctuations in the overall reserve position of each
country. The Fund's overall resources would thus increase as the
overall level of world reserves increases. Most of all, however, the
increase in Fund minimum deposit requirements would concentrate
on the countries which currently develop net surpluses and whose
currency is therefore most needed for international settlements. This
flexibility should be contrasted with the rigidity, arbitrariness, and
wastefulness of the present quota system which can be changed only
infrequently and only through a laborious process of international
renegotiation and of new national legislation on the part of all
Fund members.

One question remains to be solved. What would be the minimum
deposit requirements needed to ensure the Fund adequate lending

7. Since such subscriptions cannot now be used freely for payment by the subscriber,
but merely give him a right to apply for Fund borrowings, many countries do not
regard their creditor position with the Fund as part of their reserves. Subscriptions to,
and claims on, the Fund must then be financed by the Government itself, either out
of accumulated funds or through borrowings from its Central Bank or from the
market.

power and ensure that this lending power remain fully multilateral, *i.e.* unhampered by the development of any particular currency "scarcity" in the Fund?

Tables 18 and 19 present hypothetical calculations based on a 20 per cent level of reserve requirements. Gross reserves ($56 billion) exclude creditor countries' claims on EPU (about $1.4 billion), funded under the EPU liquidation agreement. They include, however, members' net claims on the IMF, as these would be transformed into fully liquid reserve deposits with the Fund as a result of the reform proposed here. Countries would thus be required initially to hold in deposit with the Fund an amount of about $11 billion. This would increase year by year by 20 per cent of the new additions to members' gross reserves, and would be amply sufficient to cover all prospective Fund lending for many years to come. Some increase in this required reserve ratio might ultimately prove desirable, but it is highly probable that voluntary deposits would by then be so large as to make such a compulsory increase unnecessary in practice.

These minimum requirements may be compared with the revised Fund quotas soon to come into operation and which they are designed to replace. They are considerably smaller for most countries— and particularly for those with low reserves—and only slightly larger for a few countries with very high reserves: the United States ($380 million), Germany ($290 million), Italy ($200 million), Switzerland ($410 million), Venezuela ($190 million), Portugal ($140 million),[8] Austria ($60 million), etc. They would be somewhat higher, however, for most countries than the 25 per cent gold portion of their subscription to the Fund, but it should be noted once more that the sums held in deposit with the Fund would retain their fully liquid character and be as, or more, usable in settlements as the portion of their reserves now held by most countries in the form of dollar or sterling balances.

In order to satisfy these minimum reserve requirements, all countries would have to transfer to the Fund equivalent amounts of assets. Three types of assets would be eligible for this purpose:

1. net creditor claims previously accumulated on the Fund; these would automatically be transformed into IMF deposits;

2. other liquid or semi-liquid foreign exchange holdings, *i.e.* primarily dollar and sterling balances;

3. gold.

8. Before the recent accession of Portugal to the IMF.

TABLE 18

Comparison of Minimum IMF Deposits with Revised Quotas
on the Basis of Monetary Reserves at the End of 1958

(*in millions of U.S. dollars*)

| | Gross Reserves | | | | Minimum Fund Deposits (5=20% of 4) | Revised Quotas | Excess Foreign Exchange (7=1+2-5) | Gold Payment (8=5-1-2) |
| | Net Claim on IMF | Foreign Exchange | Gold | Total (4=1+2+3) | | | | |
	(1)	(2)	(3)	(4)	(5)	(6)	(7)	(8)
I. United States	1,958	—	20,582	22,540	4,508	4,125	—	2,550
II. United Kingdom ..	—	255	2,850	3,105	621	1,950	—	366
III. Continental OEEC ...	367	6,456	9,694	16,517	3,303	3,211.0	3,962	442
A. *European Community* .	*318*	*4,660*	*6,647*	*11,625*	*2,325*	*2,610.0*	*2,816*	*163*
Germany .	147	2,587	2,639	5,373	1,075	787.5	1,659	—
France . .	—	448	602	1,050	210	787.5	238	—
Italy . .	45	1,230	1,086	2,361	472	270.0	803	—
Netherlands	69	338	1,050	1,457	291	412.5	116	—
Belgium-Luxembourg	57	57	1,270	1,384	277	352.5	—	163
B. *Other* . . .	*49*	*1,796*	*3,047*	*4,892*	*978*	*601.0*	*1,146*	*279*
Switzerland	x	132	1,925	2,057	411	x	—	279
Portugal .	x	216	493	708	142	x	74	—
Austria . .	12	464	194	670	134	75.0	342	—
Sweden . .	25	267	204	496	99	150.0	193	—
Norway .	12	200	43	255	51	100.0	161	—
Denmark .	—	199	31	230	46	130.0	153	—
Turkey . .	—	154	144	297	59	86.0	95	—
Greece . .	—	164	13	177	35	60.0	129	—
IV. Canada . . .	90	870	1,078	2,038	408	550.00	552	—
V. Latin America	40	1,376	1,742	3,158	632	1,049.50	793	9
Venezuela .	4	331	720	1,055	211	22.50	124	—
Brazil . .	—	140	325	465	93	225.00	47	—
Cuba . . .	—	293	80	373	75	100.00	218	—
Mexico . .	22	229	143	394	79	135.00	172	—
Argentina .	—	72	60	132	26	225.00	46	—
Uruguay .	4	30	180	214	43	22.50	—	9
Colombia .	—	89	72	161	32	75.00	57	—
Chile . . .	—	19	40	59	12	75.00	7	—
Guatemala .	1	21	27	49	10	15.00	12	—
Dominican Republic .	2	33	12	47	9	15.00	26	—
Panama .	—	48	—	48	10	0.75	38	—
Costa Rica	1	17	2	20	4	7.50	14	—
Ecuador .	2	14	22	38	8	15.00	8	—
Peru . . .	—	12	19	31	6	37.50	6	—
Honduras .	2	8	—	10	2	11.25	8	—
El Salvador	2	6	31	39	8	11.25	—	—
Nicaragua .	—	6	1	7	1	11.25	5	—
Paraguay .	—	7	—	7	1	11.25	6	—
Bolivia . .	—	1	1	2	—	22.50	3	—
Haiti . . .	—	—	1	2	—	11.25	—	—

TABLE 18   (*Continued*)
Comparison of Minimum IMF Deposits with Revised Quotas
on the Basis of Monetary Reserves at the End of 1958
(*in millions of U.S. dollars*)

	Gross Reserves				Minimum Fund Deposits (5=20% of 4)	Revised Quotas	Excess Foreign Exchange (7=1+2-5)	Gold Payment (8=5-1-2)
	Net Claim on IMF (1)	Foreign Exchange (2)	Gold (3)	Total (4=1+2+3) (4)	(5)	(6)	(7)	(8)
VI. Outer Sterling Area	22	3,692	755	4,469	894	1,403.0	2,820	—
Australia .	8	958	162	1,128	226	300.0	740	—
India . . .	—	475	247	722	144	600.0	331	—
Malaya . .	1	493	—	494	99	37.5	395	—
Ghana . .	—	448	—	448	90	35.0	358	—
Iraq . . .	2	255	34	291	58	12.0	199	—
Ireland . .	4	244	18	266	53ʻ	45.0	195	—
South Africa	—	105	211	317	63ˑ	150.0	42	—
Pakistan .	3	209	49	261	52	150.0	160	—
New Zealand	x	153	33	187	37	x	116	—
Ceylon . .	4	172	—	176	35	45.0	141	—
Burma . .	—	119	—	119	24	22.5	95	—
Jordan . .	—	46	—	46	9	4.5	37	—
Iceland . .	—	15	1	16	3	1.5	12	—
VII. Other	106	3,102	1,159	4,367	873	2,221.5	2,340	5
A. *Europe* . .	19	257	109	386	77	297.0	199	—
Finland . .	9	214	35	259	52	57.0	171	—
Spain . .	10	10	57	77	15	150.0	5	—
Yugoslavia	—	33	17	50	10	90.0	23	—
B. *Other* . . .	87	2,845	1,050	3,982	796	1,924.50	2,141	5
Japan . .	62	807	54	923	185	500.00	684	—
Egypt . .	—	255	174	429	86	90.00	165	—
Thailand .	3	203	112	319	66	45.00	140	—
Iran . . .	—	112	141	253	51	52.50	61	—
Indonesia .	—	180	37	217	43	165.00	137	—
Belgian Congo . .	x	138	83	221	44	x	94	—
Viet-Nam .	3	154	5	162	32	18.75	130	—
Korea . .	3	145	2	149	30	18.75	118	—
Taiwan . .	—	102	9	111	22	825.00	80	—
Lebanon .	1	16	91	108	22	6.75	—	5
Israel . .	2	91	2	94	19	25.00	74	—
Philippines	—	82	10	92	18	22.50	64	—
Ethiopia .	1	52	4	57	11	15.00	42	—
Syria . . .	2	7	24	32	6	9.75	3	—
Other . .	10	501	302	813	163	130.50	348	—
VIII. Total	2,583	15,751	37,860	56,194	1i,239	14,510	10,467	3,372

Sources and Notes: Revised estimates are based on the latest reports for 1958 published in the October 1959 issue of *International Financial Statistics*, and supplemented for French, Japanese, and Greek gold estimates by calculations based on *Federal Reserve Bulletin* statistics. As explained in the text, claims on EPU are deducted from, and net claims on the IMF added to, these IFS estimates.

The revised quotas are estimated on the basis of a uniform 50 per cent increase expert for the countries reported in September 1959 as having already agreed to the cgarle increases open to them under the Fund's resolution.

Iraq is no longer a member of the sterling area.

If we assume that all countries would initially prefer to hold onto their gold assets, most of them would satisfy fully their reserve obligation by transferring to the Fund only part of their present foreign exchange holdings. Only a handful of countries—primarily the United States and the United Kingdom—would have to transfer gold to the Fund in order to fulfill their deposit obligation (see column 8).

Table 19 shows the new balance sheet of the Fund after all such transfers have taken place. Nearly half of the Fund assets (4.9 billion) would be in gold, and the rest in various claims on member countries, but very largely in U.S. dollars (probably more than $3 billion) and in pounds sterling (probably close to $2 billion). There would be

TABLE 19

Hypothetical IMF Balance Sheet at End of 1958 after Proposed Reform
(*in billions of U.S. dollars*)

Assets		Liabilities	
1. *Gold*	4.9	1. Members' minimum deposits	
a. December 31, 1958 holdings	1.5	on current account . . .	11.2
b. New deposits	3.4	a. from members' net claims	
		on December 31, 1958 .	2.6
2. *Claims on Members* . . .	6.3	b. from additional gold and	
a. December 31, 1958 . .	1.1	foreign exchange deposits	8.7
b. New deposits	5.1	2. Net earnings	0.02
Total	11.2	*Total*	11.2

Note: Based on Table 18 above on the assumption that countries maintain only the minimum required deposits with the Fund and transfer gold to the Fund for this purpose only insofar as their foreign exchange reserves are insufficient to feed such required deposits.

no reason to change the present repayment provisions covering existing Fund claims (about $1 billion) arising from past operations. Provision would have to be made, however, with regard to the new claims acquired by the Fund as a result of the proposed reform. The bulk of these claims would be in the form of bank deposits, acceptances, and Treasury bills now held by member countries in New York or London as part of their monetary reserves. The Fund would have no immediate need to modify these investments, but should be empowered to do so, in a smooth and progressive manner, insofar as useful for the conduct of its own operations. This purpose would be served by giving the Fund an option to liquidate such investments at a maximum pace of, let us say, 5 per cent a year. The maximum yearly liability for repayment which this would entail for the United States and the United Kingdom would be of the order of $150 million and $100 million respectively.[9]

This pattern of Fund assets should rule out in practice any real danger of a "currency scarcity" in the Fund and guarantee therefore the full and continued convertibility of Fund deposits into any currencies needed by members. Currency sales by the Fund would be credited to the deposit accounts of the countries whose currency had been sold, and the large gold holdings of the Fund (nearly $5 billion) would enable it to meet any request by such members to convert into gold the excess of their deposits above their 20 per cent minimum requirement.[10] Moreover, countries which are in debt to the Fund should not have an absolute right to such conversions. The Fund could, in such cases, insist upon extraordinary amortization of their debts to it as an alternative to gold repayments susceptible of jeopardizing its own liquidity. This would also constitute an additional safeguard against any scarcity of the two major currencies in world trade and settlements—the U.S. dollar and the pound sterling—in view of the large initial holdings (more than $5 billion) of these two currencies by the Fund.

Fund Absorption of Residual Foreign Exchange Reserves

The operations described above would absorb and consolidate a substantial portion (about $5 billion) of the foreign exchange reserves of member countries, but would still leave outstanding about $10 billion of such national currency reserves. In order to eliminate fully from the international monetary system the absurdities and dangers denounced above,[11] these national currency reserves should also be converted into international Fund deposits, and all member countries should undertake to hold henceforth all of their reserves exclusively in gold and Fund deposits, except possibly for small working balances in actively traded currencies. If this were done, the

9. If a faster rate of repayment were deemed desirable, the 5 per cent option might be made to apply either to the debt itself—as suggested in the text—or to the excess of the country's gold reserves over a "normal" amount defined by the average ratio of world reserves to world imports. This second criterion would leave the United Kingdom's obligation unchanged, but would raise to about $750 million initially the annual repayment liability of the United States.

10. The minimum deposit requirement itself would, of course, rise by 20 per cent of the amount credited to the member's account since such amounts would increase correspondingly the country's gross monetary reserves.

11. See pp. 87–90.

Fund's initial deposit liabilities, estimated above at about $11 billion, would rise to approximately $21 billion, and its foreign exchange holdings to $16 billion. Its gold reserve would initially be left unaffected, at about $5 billion, or a little less than 25 per cent of total liabilities. This might be deemed uncomfortably low and entail a possible danger that the Fund might have insufficient gold to procure for its members a currency in strong demand in the event that the issuing country insisted on converting into gold any Fund deposits accruing to it in excess of its 20 per cent deposit requirement.

Such a danger, however, would be more remote than one might think. First of all, it could hardly materialize as far as the two major currencies in world trade and payments are concerned. The Fund would now hold indeed close to $9 billion in U.S. dollars and more than $5 billion in pounds sterling.[12] A strong world demand for dollars or sterling should be met, in large part, by extraordinary amortization of this indebtedness rather than by equivalent gold settlement by the Fund of the balances accruing to these two countries beyond their 20 per cent deposit requirement.

The danger of an excessive depletion of the Fund's gold resources could thus come only from two other sources:

1. direct conversion into gold of the Fund balances acquired in exchange for the initial transfer to the Fund of the foreign currency balances now held by members; or alternatively;

2. a similar conversion into gold by the countries—other than the United States and the United Kingdom—whose subsequent overall surpluses are settled through transfers of Fund balances from the deficit countries' account to the surplus countries' account.

The first of these two dangers could be warded off as far as sterling balances—but not dollar balances—are concerned by providing that the conversion of national currency balances into Fund balances should not entitle their holders to claim gold from the Fund if the balances so transferred did not entitle them to claim gold from the country on which these balances were held. This would not impair in any way the convertibility of these Fund balances into all and any currencies actually needed by their holders in international settlements, nor the gold exchange guarantee and other privileges attach-

12. Official dollar balances of foreign countries were reported at $8,665 million at the end of 1958, and total—official and private—U.S. Government bonds and notes at $983 million. Non-colonial sterling balances were estimated at about $6.9 billion. On the basis of the 1957 ratio of official to private sterling balances. this might be broken down roughly into $5.3 billion of official balances and $1.5 billion of private balances.

ing to Fund balances in general. What it would mean is that the right to claim gold from the Fund would attach only to the Fund balances exceeding the sum of the country's normal 20 per cent requirement *plus* the balances initially acquired in exchange for gold-inconvertible national currency balances. This second limitation, moreover, would be eliminated gradually as the debtors of such balances— primarily the United Kingdom—amortized their corresponding indebtedness to the Fund.

The only residual danger of an excessive depletion of the Fund's gold assets would then arise from the conversion into gold of deposits at the Fund transferred to overall surplus countries other than the United States and the United Kingdom. Let us note, however, that only 80 per cent, at most, of such transfers would expose the Fund to gold payments since 20 per cent of them would increase the minimum deposit requirements of the receiving countries. Secondly, the option of the Fund to claim annual amortization instalments from the debtors of the balances could be exercised, whenever necessary, and bring in up to $1 billion a year of additional gold resources to the Fund.[13]

The danger of a gold or currency scarcity in the Fund would thus appear extremely remote, especially as most countries could be expected to hold Fund deposits well in excess of their minimum requirements. Convenience and earning incentives have so far prompted countries other than the United States and the United Kingdom to retain, on the average, more than half—rather than merely 20 per cent—of their gross reserves in foreign exchange rather than gold.[14] They will have, in any case, to retain some working balances in a form other than gold in order to avoid repeated gold sales or purchases each time they wish to sell or buy foreign currencies in the market to stabilize their own exchange rate. These working balances will have to be held either as excess deposits with the Fund, or directly in the key currencies actively traded on the exchange markets. Either of these two alternatives would reduce substantially the danger of an excessive gold drain from the Fund. Working bal-

13. Under the formula described on p. 111 above, this option would normally apply to 5 per cent of the total currency balances (about $15 billion) transferred to the Fund, *i.e.* $750 million. It could, however, also be applied, alternatively, to 5 per cent of the excess of the debtor's gross reserves over and above the average ratio of world reserves to world imports. This would raise initially by about $300 million the annual repayment liability of the United States.

14. See Table 12 above.

ances equal to only 5 per cent of annual imports, for instance, would absorb as much as $5 billion.

All in all, therefore, the absorption and consolidation of all outstanding foreign exchange reserves—with the possible exception of moderate working balances—into Fund deposits would appear feasible, even on the basis of the 20 per cent minimum deposit requirement envisaged up to now. Yet, provision would have to be made to safeguard the Fund's liquidity both against unforeseen conversions of excess deposits into gold and, in the long run, against the increasing gap between the probable level of world gold stocks and the desirable expansion of overall monetary reserves. Three different techniques might be used—either alternatively, or in combination—to meet both problems. The simplest one would be for the Fund to issue medium-term gold certificates, payable either in gold or in excess Fund deposits, and carrying a higher rate of interest than liquid Fund deposits. Such certificates should be particularly attractive to high reserve holders. The second possibility would be to authorize the Fund to raise uniformly the 20 per cent deposit requirement to a higher ratio—25 per cent or 30 per cent, for instance—of each country's gross monetary reserves. The third would be to leave the basic 20 per cent requirement unchanged—or to increase it more moderately—but to impose higher deposit requirements upon that portion of each member's reserves which exceeds the average ratio of world monetary gold to world imports.

Any increase in the compulsory deposit obligation initially accepted by members should normally require a qualified majority (two-thirds, three-fourths, or even four-fifths) of the Fund's total voting power. If, however, such a majority could not be reached at a time when a real gold scarcity develops in the Fund, such a "gold scarcity" would have to be declared by the Fund and entail the automatic adoption of either the second or the third of the three solutions discussed above, to the extent necessary to preserve the Fund's ability to meet its gold conversion commitments. If this provision for automatic quota increases in such a case proved unnegotiable, a less satisfactory, but still workable, alternative might be envisaged. Any country would be recognized the right to refuse such an increase in its deposit obligation, but with the proviso that the exercise of this right would automatically entail the "scarcity" of that particular country's currency in the sense of Article VII of the present Fund

Agreement, and carry the consequences envisaged in that Article.[15] As different from the present—and politically inapplicable—procedure, however, such a declaration would be left to the discretion of the country concerned rather than of the Fund. In fact, our previous discussion makes it abundantly clear that such a contingency would be most unlikely to arise, at least for many years to come, and that confidence in Fund deposits should by that time be sufficiently strong to avert any such decision on the part of any country.

Clearing and Lending Operations of the Fund

As indicated above,[16] the major safeguard against an inflationary level of Fund lending would lie in the overall limitations placed on the net increase of the Fund's loans during any twelve months period.

These loans should fall into two broad categories, similar in many respects to those of national central banks' credit operations:

1. advances or rediscounts, undertaken at the initiative of the borrowing country;

2. open market operations, or investments, undertaken at the initiative of the Fund itself.

The normal procedures for Fund advances need not differ substantially from those gradually developed by the Fund over its twelve years of existence. They should be subordinated to full agreement between the Fund and the member with relation not only to the maturity of the loan, but also to the broad economic and financial policies followed by the member to ensure long run equilibrium in its international transactions without excessive recourse to trade and exchange restrictions. The recent stand-by techniques of lending might, in addition, be supplemented by overdraft agreements, to be renewed at frequent intervals, and guaranteeing all members in good standing rapid and automatic Fund assistance in case of need, but for modest amounts and with short-term repayment provisions. These overdraft agreements would be primarily designed to give time for full consideration of a request for normal, medium-term, loans or stand-by agreements, and would be guaranteed by the country's minimum deposit obligation.

The only basic difference between the new lending procedures and the ones now in existence is that the proposed structure of Fund

15. See also p. 11
16. Pp. 103–104

operations would eliminate one of the most puzzling requirements of the present Articles of Agreement. Article V, Section 3, Subsection (a) provides that "A member shall be entitled to buy *the currency of another member* from the Fund in exchange for *its own currency* subject to the following conditions: (i) The member desiring to purchase *the currency* represents that *it* is presently needed for making *in that currency* payments which are consistent with the provisions of the Agreement." [17]

This is very bizarre indeed and raises at least two broad questions. First of all, it is very difficult, under convertibility conditions, to identify *any particular currency* as needed by a member. The settlement of most international transactions takes place through private sales and purchases of foreign exchange in the market and need not involve the member itself, or its monetary authorities. The latter's *need* for foreign exchange arises only when they feel impelled to intervene on the exchange markets to repurchase excess supplies of their own currency and arrest its depreciation in terms of other currencies. They do not, even then, however, need any *particular* currency for this purpose, although they will presumably tend to operate chiefly in widely traded currencies and to sell preferably those which command the highest market price—in relation to their par value or official buying rate for foreign currencies—at that particular moment.

Secondly, it should be noted that the Fund Agreement allows members to purchase foreign currencies in exchange *for their own currency*—*i.e.* in exchange for their own I.O.U.'s—but not in exchange for other foreign currencies owned or acquired by them. This means in effect that the Fund could never really fulfill effectively one of the main purposes stated in Article I, Section (iv) of the Agreement, *i.e.* "to assist in the establishment of a multilateral system of payments in respect of current transactions between members . . ." This was a major gap in the Fund Agreement and made it necessary to set up in 1950 a separate institution, the European Payments Union, to restore a multilateral system of settlements among the European countries and their associated monetary areas.[18]

17. The italics are mine.
18. The restoration of convertibility for non-residents by most major trading countries provides, as long as it lasts, an alternative machinery for the multilateralization of payments. It does not, however, dispense with the need to discourage through international cooperation and agreements later relapses into inconvertibility by a country in difficulty, nor with the need to help other countries withstand the impact of such a decision by one of their major trading partners. This is indeed one

Both of these shortcomings would be remedied by the Fund reform proposed in this study. Bilateral settlements among central banks would be obviated through the use of the Fund as a Clearing House for such settlements. Foreign currency balances acquired by a central bank would be deposited to its Fund account and debited from the account of the debtor of such balances. Any other member's currency could, conversely, be purchased by a member through corresponding debits to its own account and credits to the account of the country whose currency is bought. Finally, any loan granted by the Fund to a member would be credited to its Fund deposit account, and the member could draw on this account in any currency whatsoever without having to make any "representation" that it needs it to make payments in that particular currency.[19]

The second broad category of Fund lending would take place through investments in the financial markets of member countries. These operations would be decided very largely at the initiative of the Fund itself, but always of course in agreement with the monetary authorities of the countries concerned. Such agreement would be necessary in any case to attach to these investments the same guarantees against exchange and inconvertibility risks as those which protect the Fund's own deposit liabilities.

The first investments of this character would be imposed upon the Fund by its absorption of the outstanding national currency reserves transferred to it by members in exchange for Fund deposits. They would be overwhelmingly dollar and sterling investments and would be subject to special provisions, already outlined above, to avoid unnecessary disturbances to the monetary and financial markets of the United States and the United Kingdom. The resources derived from their progressive liquidation, however, would normally be reemployed in other markets whose need for international capital is greater than in the United States and the United Kingdom. A portion of such investments might even be channelled into relatively

---

of the major objectives of the European Monetary Agreement which replaced, at the end of last year, the European Payments Union Agreement. A further discussion of the vital issues involved may be found in my book on *Europe and the Money Muddle*, particularly pp. 113–116, 202, and 223–229.

19. This would also put an end to the kind of absurdities referred to on pp. 12–13 above, and under which Fund loans have been mostly financed so far by the country— the United States—which suffered the worst loss of reserves, and hardly or not at all by the countries whose reserves were increasing.

long-term investments for economic development through purchases of IBRD bonds or other securities of a similar character.

A primary consideration in determining the pattern of Fund investments would be the need to preserve the full liquidity of its members' deposits. It should be noted, however, that the Fund would be in a particularly strong position in this respect as the total amount of its required deposits—initially some $11 billion—could hardly decline in practice, but would on the contrary grow year by year with the increase of world reserves. Any withdrawals of deposits by members whose overall reserves are declining would be more than matched by increases in the required deposits of members whose reserves are increasing.[20] The liquidity problem of the Fund would be very largely confined to the preservation of the convertibility of its excess deposits into any currency needed in payment, and, eventually, into gold if their holders requested it. This problem has already been amply discussed above and need not detain us further.

A number of other interesting suggestions relating to the Fund's lending procedures have recently been presented by Mr. Maxwell Stamp,[21] former Advisor to the Governors of the Bank of England, British Alternate Executive Director of the Fund from 1951 to 1953, and Director of the Fund's European Department from 1953 to 1954. Mr. Stamp would also favor the channelling of part of the IMF credits through the IBRD, through the International Finance Corporation, and even through private corporations. He also proposes to explore further the possibility of using collateral pledges of commercial bills, Treasury bills, tax revenues, etc. as guarantees of the Fund's loans,

20. The theoretical possibility of a decline in the monetary reserves of all countries taken together should, however, be noted in passing. The only case on record is that of the first years of the great depression when world reserves declined by about $2 billion from 1928 to 1932 as a result of the wholesale liquidation of their foreign exchange assets by central banks. The above proposals are precisely designed to ward off the repetition of a similar collapse of the gold exchange standard. Overall world reserves could also decline through large-scale sales of official reserves to private holders, reversing the trend of at least the last forty years of monetary history. Article 4 (f) of the European Payments Union Agreement provided that "Each Contracting Party shall use its best endeavors to ensure that abnormal balances in the currencies of other Contracting Parties are not held by banks other than central banks or otherwise placed so that they are excluded from the calculation of bilateral surpluses or deficits." A similar provision should be written in the new Fund Agreement to prevent countries from eluding their minimum deposit requirement by excessive transfers of international reserves to private banks.

21. Maxwell Stamp, "The Fund and the Future," in *Lloyds Bank Review*, October 1958, pp. 1–20.

and favors a more active and flexible use of the interest rates as an instrument of policy. The other parts of Mr. Stamp's article and the suggestions presented by Sir Oliver Franks in his 1958 annual statement to the shareholders of Lloyds Bank rejoin very largely the proposals developed in the present study and previously outlined in *Europe and the Money Muddle.*

Other Suggestions

The acceptance of the basic reforms proposed above should eliminate all existing balance of payments grounds for permissible discrimination under the GATT. This should constitute a powerful incentive for U.S. support of these proposals, as the United States has long been the main target of such discrimination by other countries.

The gradual liberalization of remaining trade, exchange and tariff restrictions could also be given a new impetus by these reforms if they were allied to a continuous and world-wide negotiation of *reciprocal* liberalization commitments, similar to that successfully undertaken regionally by the OEEC on the basis of the EPU Agreement. Prospective credit assistance by the Fund to countries in difficulty should help spur the acceptance and implementation of such commitments by members. Yet, the OEEC experience also suggests that members will insist on retaining the right to invoke escape clauses whenever such assistance is either insufficient or inappropriate to meet their deficits. As in OEEC, a joint examination of the overall policies followed by the member should be undertaken in such cases and lead to agreed proposals for monetary rehabilitation and stabilization and for the restoration of the liberalization measures reciprocally accepted by all Fund members. Ideally, the Fund should be given the right to disallow, after one year for instance, continued recourse to such escape clauses if it deems them to be no longer justified. Such a decision might entail automatically the right for the country in question to allow fluctuations in its exchange rate as long as its gross reserves remain inferior to, let us say, 30 per cent of annual imports.

Finally, some fundamental reforms in the cumbersome administrative machinery of the Fund have long been overdue. Greater efforts should be made to preserve effective contacts at all levels between the Fund and the national administrations of its members. Periodic meetings of high-level representatives, currently entrusted with monetary policy in their own country, should determine the broad lines of the Fund's policy and the limits within which decisions can be delegated to permanent representatives or to the Fund's management itself. The OEEC and EPU experience should serve as an invaluable guide in shaping up such reforms in more concrete terms.

These, and other questions, could not be fruitfully explored within the scope of the present study.[22] Actual possibilities for agreement can only be discovered through the process of international negotiation itself. The results of such a negotiation would certainly differ, in many respects, from the proposals outlined above. It is probable that the final compromises that prove initially feasible on a world-wide scale will remain substantially short of the broad and bold aims and techniques suggested here, and of what might be agreed to within smaller groups of countries, more closely interdependent on one another, keenly conscious of this interdependence, and more willing to trust one another's policies and commitments. I shall thus consider below the way in which the agreements which prove feasible on a world-wide level could be supported and supplemented by regional agreements of a similar, or more ambitious, nature, particularly among the OEEC and the EEC countries. This discussion will be far briefer, however, as it involves very largely a mere adaptation to a more limited geographical framework of the suggestions outlined above, and as I have already developed elsewhere in greater detail the possible shape of future European monetary cooperation and integration.[23]

22. See *Europe and the Money Muddle*, pp. 109–138 and 294–301.
23. See particularly: "Système et Politique Monétaires de l'Europe Fédérée," *Economia Internazionale*, Vol. VI, No. 1, Genoa, 1953; *The Future of the European Payments System*, Wicksell Lectures, May 1958, Stockholm; and "La Monnaie et le Marché Commun—Politiques Nationales et Intégration Régionale," *Cahiers de l'Institut de Science Economique Appliquée*, No. 74, December 1958, Paris.

CHAPTER 5

Regional Monetary Cooperation in OEEC

The outstanding success of the European Payments Union in help-
ing its members move from bilateralism to convertibility or near-
convertibility was eloquently demonstrated by the joint convertibility
decisions of last December. Paradoxically enough, this very success
sounded the death knell of the EPU itself. It did, however, bring out
very suddenly from the limbo where it was waiting for the sound of
the convertibility trumpets the European Monetary Agreement la-
boriously negotiated three and one-half years earlier among the
seventeen countries of the OEEC.

The European Monetary Agreement

The EMA constitutes an imaginative attempt to preserve into the
convertibility era some of the elements of the regional monetary cooperation previously embodied in the EPU Agreement. This required drastic and long overdue readjustments in the EPU machinery.

First and foremost, bilateral accounts among central banks had
long ceased to provide a valid and automatic criterion of a country's
borrowing needs or lending ability. The EPU system of so-called
automatic credits was therefore abandoned and replaced by provisions for discretionary credits, financed by a European Fund of
$600 million.

The second, and most intricate, part of the European Monetary
Agreement consisted in a complete overhauling of the multilateral
system for settlements initially established by EPU. This system
involved the full and automatic compensation, at the end of each
month, of all debts and claims accumulated during the month by
each member country vis-à-vis each of the others, and their consolidation into a single net debt or net claim vis-à-vis the EPU itself, which

121

was then settled partly through EPU credit accounts and partly through gold or dollar transfers. In the early days of EPU, the balances notified to the Agent at the end of each month by the European central banks had been accumulated by them during the month under the operation of bilateral payments agreements eschewing all private transactions on the exchange markets. Free exchange markets had been gradually reopened in the intervening years, however, and multilateral arbitrage agreements substituted in most cases for bilateral payments agreements. By 1958 the largest portion of the balances communicated monthly to the Agent thus resulted from the stabilization interventions of central banks in the market rather than from direct bookkeeping transactions between them. The European Monetary Agreement registered explicitly this evolution, while still leaving room for bilateral agreements with the few countries whose currencies remained technically inconvertible.

The crucial change introduced by EMA in the EPU system of multilateral settlements lay in the fact that the central banks are no longer required to bring into the monthly compensations all the balances acquired during the month. They may, at their own discretion, bring such balances into compensation or retain them as part of their monetary reserves. Some change of this sort was, of course, well nigh unavoidable as a consequence of the restoration of convertibility in Europe. One could hardly allow European central banks to retain convertible U.S. dollars or other non-member currencies, but forbid them to keep convertible pounds or Deutsche marks as a component of their monetary reserves. Yet this return to a multi-currency gold exchange standard carries with it very real dangers for future monetary convertibility and trade liberalization. Now as in the 1920's, sudden shifts from one currency into another or into gold may endanger the position of the key currencies actually used as foreign exchange reserves by central banks. Moreover, some countries might again, when they run into difficulties, be tempted to use promises of trade concessions or threats of trade restrictions as a weapon to induce other countries to accumulate their currency or to spend it exclusively within their own currency area.

The chief contributions to European monetary cooperation retained in the EMA are its moderate provisions for short or medium term balance of payments credits[1] and, most of all, the provision of

---

1. In addition to the European Fund loans already mentioned, members also undertake to grant each other, under the name of "interim finance," small overdraft facilities repayable within the month.

an exchange rate guarantee, in terms of the U.S. dollar, for all foreign exchange balances accumulated by members in the currencies of other members. This indeed is the main practical significance of the multilateral settlements machinery theoretically salvaged by EMA from the EPU Agreement. Each country must notify official buying and selling rates for its currency in terms of the U.S. dollar, valid until further notice, and at which it undertakes to settle at the end of each month the net balance of the bilateral claims or debts reported by members for settlement. These rates may be modified at any time by the country concerned, but, in this case, the claims and debts outstanding at the time of the change will be settled on the basis of the rates previously in force. This is, in practice, the only reason which members might have to make use of the EMA machinery for settlements, since in all other cases the official buying and selling rates at which the EMA operates would be less favorable to them than the rates at which the currencies in question could be bought or sold instead on the exchange market.[2]

Proposals for a European Clearing House or Reserve Fund

The European Monetary Agreement should primarily be regarded as an invaluable, if limping, compromise between conflicting points of view as to the future monetary organization of Europe. Many of its shortcomings bear the marks of past, rather than current, divergencies of views between the United Kingdom and some of its main partners on the Continent. Britain was toying in 1955 with the idea of establishing a flexible exchange rate for the pound or, at least, widening considerably the margin between buying and selling rates. Its main opponent on this point, as well as on others, was Switzerland. The United Kingdom's authorities seem now to be satisfied with exchange rate stability and narrow exchange margins, and Switzerland has become the main ally of the United Kingdom in its differences with the European Economic Community over the formation of a European Free Trade Area.

In view of these fundamental changes in member countries'

2. No balances indeed were reported for settlement in the first monthly operations (for January 1959), except by four countries still operating under bilateral payments agreements. Net payments totalled only about $2 million, as compared with $300 million in the last month of EPU's operations.

The above summary of the European Monetary Agreement is a highly condensed and simplified one. For a fuller account, see the official text and accompanying memorandum of the Secretary General of OEEC—released by OEEC in August 1955 —and my own discussion in *Europe and the Money Muddle*, pp. 220–233 and 280–284.

policies, the 1955 European Monetary Agreement would hardly have
been put into operation in December 1958 without substantial revisions, except for a series of unforeseen events which left little time
or hope for a successful renegotiation. A fundamental, and long
overdue, revision of the EPU Agreement had been repeatedly postponed pending the results of the Free Trade Area discussions. When
the latter finally collapsed in December, the maintenance of EPU in
its then existing form became more anachronistic than ever, but the
liquidation of EPU automatically entailed, under the 1955 Agreement, the simultaneous entry into force of the European Monetary
Agreement. Final action was precipitated by the French decision to
readjust and stabilize their own monetary and exchange system,
preparatory to the first round of tariff and trade liberalization of the
European Economic Community on January 1, 1959.

This hurried time table and the bitter atmosphere resulting from
the breakdown of the Free Trade Area talks precluded any further
negotiation of an EPU or EMA revision at that time. Yet, the need
for such a revision had been clearly affirmed in all the Maudling
Committee discussions. The EPU Managing Board had been in-
structed to explore the problem, and had already presented pre-
liminary reports to the full committee. There is little or no doubt
that the present EMA system will require substantial modifications
if and when the European Economic Community and the other
OEEC members succeed in patching up their differences, and agree
on some new form of economic association among the seventeen
OEEC countries. The mutual commitments to be undertaken by
members in the trade field would be more ambitious than those of the
OEEC Code of Liberalization, and would have to be supported by
correspondingly strong commitments in the money and payments
field.

The keystone of such a reform of the present EMA would bear a
close similarity to the proposals advanced above for the reform of the
IMF. The project would be regional, rather than world-wide in
scope, however, and could probably be negotiated and implemented
more easily, more rapidly and more fully within such a framework.

The participating countries would establish jointly a Clearing
House centralizing all payments among their separate central banks.
These payments would be effected through corresponding debits and
credits to the account maintained by each central bank with the
Clearing House.

These clearing accounts would be fed, first of all, by the compulsory transfer to each country's account of any and all balances
in another member's currency purchased from the market by its
central bank or credited to it by another central bank. They could
be fed, in addition, by transfers of gold, or convertible currencies
of third countries, or even of other currencies specified by the Clearing in the light of its members' current demand for such currencies.
The first of these two provisions would be designed both to simplify
payments among members and to prevent any relapse into open or
concealed bilateralism among them.

The clearing accounts would, of course, be fully convertible and
could be freely drawn upon by their holders to make payments to
third countries as well as to member countries. They would, moreover, carry an exchange guarantee in terms of a jointly agreed unit
of account. This unit might, as in the case of the IMF, be defined
merely and simply in terms of gold. A less rigid, and on the whole
preferable, procedure might be to revive a unit similar to the former
EPU unit of account, *i.e.* tantamount in effect to an exchange
guarantee in terms of whichever European currency will in fact
remain stablest in the future with respect to gold itself.[3]

The participating countries might be required, at least initially,
to maintain in their clearing account a minimum balance equivalent
to, let us say, 10 or 20 per cent of their total gold and foreign
exchange reserves. Based on current reserve levels, these required
balances would total today as much as $2 billion if a 10 per cent
"reserve requirement" were adopted. The resources thus placed at
the disposal of the Clearing would be totally unaffected by intra-
European disequilibria, since any decrease in some countries' global

3. Such a clause would have the same effect as a gold guarantee unless *all* member
currencies modified *in the same direction*—upward or downward—their present parity
with respect to gold. The application of a straight gold clause in such an event would
probably result in unjustified windfall losses or gains for the debtors and creditors in
the Clearing. It might be noted that the elimination of the EPU unit of account by
EMA and its substitution by a gold clause for some transactions and a dollar clause
for others would open a serious and unsolved question in the improbable event of a
change in the United States gold price or gold policy. A whole article (Article 14), entitled "Modification in the United States Price or Policy for Gold," is devoted to this
very problem, but its call for an urgent and comprehensive review of the Agreement in
such a case is only a thin disguise for a total lack of agreement at this stage as to the
way in which the situation should be handled. The needless introduction of such
complications and uncertainties in the Agreement is difficult to explain except on the
basis of British fears that the EPU unit of account might enjoy greater prestige than
the pound sterling, displacing it gradually as a key currency in world trade and payments.

reserves and minimum deposits would then be exactly offset by corresponding increases in other members' reserves and required deposits. The resources of the Clearing would fall only as a consequence of global deficits of the OEEC area as a whole toward the rest of the world, and even then by only 10 per cent of the amount of such deficits. A cumulative deficit of $10 billion would be necessary, for instance, to reduce by one half the funds initially placed at the disposal of the Clearing. Such an evolution would be highly improbable, and would in any case call for joint readjustment policies in order to harmonize the European pace of monetary and credit expansion with that of other areas, or for preserving a desirable pace of expansion against the impact of outside deflation through the negotiation of foreign credits or through an increase of restrictions on trade and payments with non-member countries.

The resources of the Clearing would be held primarily in gold and convertible foreign currencies, so as to enable it to maintain the world-wide convertibility of its members' accounts. The factors of stability underlined above, however, would make it possible for the Clearing—just as for any bank—to reinvest at short or medium term, within or outside the OEEC area, a reasonable portion of its assets without endangering thereby the effective liquidity of its deposits for their individual holders.

The lending procedures of the Clearing would follow the same general pattern outlined above with respect to the IMF. The criteria determining the overall amount of such lending, however, would be different, and far less automatic in character. The total amount of assistance provided to members would have to be adjusted in the light of the current inflationary or deflationary pressures within the area and of the evolution of the balance of payments and monetary reserves of the group as a whole toward the outside world. This would not, of course, ensure that the policies of the group as a whole would be wiser than those of other countries or than those which would have been independently followed otherwise by its national member states. The group's policies might be more inflationary or more deflationary, as well as less inflationary or less deflationary, more foolish as well as wiser, than those pursued in the rest of the world. The choice of policies open to it would merely be wider and freer than that otherwise available to its individual members. It should certainly be exercised in such a way as to preserve freedom of trade within the area, and strengthen its ability to follow liberal policies toward the rest of the world as well. The latter result could not be guaranteed, however, in the absence of a sufficient coordination of policies and mutual financial assistance between the group and other major trading countries. Important tasks would thus continue to devolve on world-wide organizations such as GATT and the IMF, even though effective performance at that level is likely to develop more slowly and gradually than will prove feasible at the regional level.

As in the case of the IMF, the influence and means of action of the Clearing would be likely to grow at a rapid pace, as experience overcomes initial diffidence toward the system and the inertia of old habits and traditions. Its deposit accounts, particularly, might be expected to exceed largely, after a time, the minimum requirements initially adopted and even, possibly, to make these unnecessary. Those accounts should indeed prove highly attractive to member banks in view of the unique guarantees attached to them. The convertibility and exchange rate guarantees provided would eliminate the risks of unilateral inconvertibility or exchange rate devaluation inseparable from the current investment of monetary reserves in national, so-called "key" currencies. Default risks, moreover, would be practically eliminated by the obligation accepted by all members to channel through the Clearing all payments due by anyone of them to another. The overdrafts of a defaulting borrower would thus be automatically amortized by the transfers made to its account by any other member, and this procedure would not be dependent on the good faith of the borrowing country itself, but on the commitments subscribed to by all other members of the Clearing.

Finally—but only as long as the IMF reforms proposed above are not adopted—the Clearing might attract similar accounts even from central banks of non-member countries whose payments relations are largely with the EPU area. Indeed, nearly 40 per cent of non-EPU countries' merchandise imports originate in the EPU area, and this proportion exceeds 50 per cent for the countries outside the dollar-area. The European Clearing, based on a close alliance between sterling and other European currencies would tend to develop gradually into a powerful monetary center, susceptible to assume an international role comparable to that of London before 1914, but which London alone has become too weak to perform today. Non-member countries could be expected to transfer gradually into clearing accounts some portion of the national currency balances now held by them as monetary reserves. Insofar as these balances are now held in non-member currencies—*i.e.* practically in U.S. dollars—this would strengthen the gross reserve position of the Clearing and result in some further expansion of its lending capacity. Insofar as they are now held in member currencies—practically pounds sterling—it might help smooth out the impact now exercised upon the debtor of such balances—practically the United Kingdom —by fluctuations in their overall amount. The largest portion of these fluctuations would indeed be associated with the settlement of imbalance between the owners of the balances and the European area itself, and would not cause any drain on the Clearing's gold and dollar reserves, nor any change in its other assets, but merely a re-shuffling of its net claims or debts vis à vis the United Kingdom on the one hand, and its other members on the other. While persistent movements of this sort in the same direction would obviously require in the end cash settlements among the member countries concerned, a great many of them could properly be cushioned by the Clearing and help avoid or smooth out the undesirable pressures which they would otherwise exercise upon these countries' policies.

A European Clearing House would therefore be able to offer a substantial contribution to the preservation of international liquidity and to the reduction of the dangers attendant to the use of national currencies as international monetary reserves. It could not, however, solve such world-wide problems as fully and effectively as a revised IMF might do. The proposals advanced in this chapter, therefore, should not be regarded as a lasting substitute for the IMF reforms discussed in the preceding chapter. On the other hand, neither should a global IMF approach be regarded as a full substitute, making a European Clearing superfluous and useless. First of all, the setting up and implementation of a fully satisfactory IMF system will probably require several years of negotiation and experimentation. Secondly, the management of a world-wide monetary clearing system, and particularly the investment of the large funds derived from its operation, will present enormous administrative and political hurdles, which can best be surmounted through some decentralization of the Fund's decision-making process. Finally, the high degree of economic and political interdependence of the European countries[4] and their experience of past cooperation are likely to make feasible far more extensive regional trade liberalization, credit commitments and policy harmonization among them than could conceivably be negotiated and implemented on a world-wide level.

The practical feasibility of a European Clearing Agreement, however, is intimately bound up at this stage with the renewal of OEEC negotiations for a European Free Trade Area or Economic Association. Persistent conflicts of views subsist in this respect and make the final outcome highly uncertain. The French protectionist objections which contributed so much to the breakdown of past negotiations may gradually abate if the remarkable success achieved to date by the French monetary and exchange readjustments of last December are confirmed and consolidated. The resurgence of French nationalism today, and possibly of German nationalism tomorrow, may also weaken the political unity objectives of the six countries of the European Economic Community and remove other sources of opposition to a broader, but looser, European Economic Association. On the other side of the Channel, influential circles are already arguing in favor of a full-fledged accession of the United Kingdom to the European Economic Community itself, as it stands today.

None of these trends, however, is sufficiently pronounced to permit any easy prediction of future developments. The European Economic Community exists, not only through the measures and institutions provided for in the Rome Treaty, but also through the myriad of decisions taken by individuals and firms—within and outside the Community itself—to adjust their economic activity and investment plans to the new horizons opened by it. Vested interests will increasingly combine with political ideals to resist any dilution of the six countries' progress toward economic integration and federal unity.

The most realistic and constructive solution of these dilemmas would seem to lie in a parallel drive toward both sets of objectives. Whatever degree of cooperation and liberalization can in fact be achieved among the seventeen OEEC countries should be exploited to the full, but without being allowed to develop as a brake on the closer integration which can realistically be aimed at within the European Economic Community. The gradual adaptation of our legal economic institutions to the facts of international economic

4. About three-fourths of the OEEC countries' total exports are directed to each other and their overseas monetary areas.

interdependence can be carried forward most easily and successfully if we recognize the complementary—rather than the competitive— role that may be assigned to overlapping regional groupings in this respect.[5] The six countries of the Community have indicated their readiness to accept a far closer integration than would be acceptable to the seventeen countries of OEEC, just as the latter may accept broader and firmer commitments to each other than they would be ready to extend to the world at large through GATT or the IMF.

The ensuing discussion of monetary integration among the six countries of the European Economic Community is based on this philosophy. The exact line of demarcation between the institutions of the Community and those of a future European Economic Association cannot be predicted at this stage and should, in any case, fluctuate over time as the future success of integration policies prompts the acceptance of closer commitments and surrenders of sovereignty by the seventeen OEEC countries as well as by the six Community countries.

5. I have discussed these vital policy issues more fully in the last two chapters of *Europe and the Money Muddle.*

CHAPTER 6

Monetary Integration in the European Economic Community

The adoption of the IMF and EMA reforms suggested above would go a long way toward providing the European Economic Community with a stable monetary framework and facilitating the adoption of liberal policies by the Community toward the rest of Europe and toward the outside world. Yet, a number of factors, specific to the Community itself, must be taken into account for the shaping up of its future monetary policies and institutions.

First of all, the commercial commitments of members have already been negotiated and spelled out in considerable detail in the Rome Treaty, together with a number of other provisions designed to harmonize competitive conditions throughout the Community.

Secondly, these commitments are far more drastic and rigid than those which are likely to be negotiated within the broader framework of GATT or the IMF, or even of the OEEC group as a whole. Correspondingly stronger commitments in the monetary and financial fields will be necessary to ensure a coordination of the members' internal policies sufficient to preserve long run equilibrium in their balances of payments without resort to trade and exchange restrictions outlawed by the Rome Treaty.

Thirdly, a further evolution of the Community's monetary institutions may possibly be called for, in the long run, if the success of the economic integration measures already accepted encourages further progress toward political, as well as economic, integration among the six countries of the Community. The institutional framework to be adopted in the early stages of the Community's life should be flexible enough to facilitate, rather than hamper, such an evolution. On the other hand, the tasks already assigned to the Community's authorities by the Treaty of Rome are so vast and formidable as to deserve their full attention and energies in the immediate years

ahead. The most elementary wisdom and caution will warn them
against any premature injection of controversial and divisive issues
relating to hypothetical hopes and far-distant blueprints upon which
there does not exist at present a sufficient basis for agreement among
the participating countries.

The suggestions outlined below should be read in this light. Some
of them may be immediately relevant and applicable, while others
could only be negotiated and implemented if a protracted period of
successful experimentation with less ambitious aims and techniques
of integration induces the six countries to push further ahead the
gradual merging of their separate administrative and political powers
and responsibilities for monetary management.

Monetary Integration through the Disciplines of the Market

Proponents and adversaries of economic integration generally
agree on one point: a real integration presupposes the acceptance
by member countries of substantial surrenders of national sovereignty. Incontrovertible as it is, this observation also suggests a
totally misleading interpretation of the political options actually
available to the national authorities of a country. National sovereignty is always subject to stringent limitations, resulting from
economic imperatives and independent of any legal integration agreements or international commitments. One of these imperatives, of
particular relevance to the issues to be discussed presently, is the
unavoidability of overall balance in a country's external transactions.
Deficits in current account must necessarily be balanced by capital
imports, and surpluses on current account by capital exports, regardless of the national policies pursued.

The authorities of a deficit country must choose therefore among
the following alternatives. First of all, they may be able to finance
these deficits by drawing down international assets previously
accumulated by the country, but only to the extent that such assets
exist and—in the case of private assets—only insofar as their liquidation can be effectively controlled or influenced by the national
authorities. Alternatively, they may be able to finance the deficits
through the importation of foreign capital, but only within the
limits resulting from the foreign lenders' willingness to lend and
from the acceptability of the conditions, financial and political,
attached by them to these operations. The maximum size of the

current deficits will thus be unavoidably limited by the maximum size of these feasible capital imports and liquidation of assets.

Beyond this, the national authorities cannot escape limiting the deficits to the level of available finance. In the absence of any international commitments, three methods—and three methods only —will be open to them. The first will be to modify their international monetary policy—in the broadest acception of this term—in such a way as to adjust the country's overall demand for goods and services to its productive capacity *plus* the excess imports whose financing can be assured by the means outlined above. This may not suffice to restore external equilibrium at high levels of employment and economic activity if the relation of internal costs to costs abroad is such as to dampen export demand and stimulate an excessive demand for imports. The readjustment of cost disparities would require in this case either a reduction of internal cost elements—especially wages— or, more probably, a lowering of exchange rates. This may be avoided, however, at least temporarily, through export subsidies, increases in import duties, or quantitative trade and exchange restrictions.

International agreements will usually involve some sacrifice of sovereignty with respect to the use of subsidies, of tariff and other restrictions, and possibly of exchange rate readjustments. On the other hand, they will also guarantee the country against the shocks to its economy resulting from the resort to similar techniques by its trading partners. They may also enlarge the scope of available external financing through official credits, mutual aid, or merely the stimulation given to private capital imports by the guarantees provided against exchange restrictions or devaluation. The limited sacrifices of sovereignty involved in integration agreements may therefore be offset, or far more than offset, by the opportunities which they offer to protect the country's export markets and to attract additional capital to finance temporary, or desirable, deficits on current account.

This is all the more true as the internal policy readjustments which may be required for the implementation of the country's commitments to trade liberalization and exchange rate stability are in any case economically desirable and even unavoidable in the long run. Trade and exchange restrictions, and even exchange devaluation, offer only a temporary escape from the economic imperatives to which any country is subjected, irrespective of its legal international commitments. Restrictions may be used to adjust a country's import level to its export proceeds, but persistent inflationary policies would reduce the latter to a mere trickle in the end, because of their impact upon the country's internal prices and production costs. Devaluation would become inescapable at some point to restore an export level sufficient to finance even the most essential import needs. But again the internal prices increases and external currency depreciation brought about by a failure to readjust persistent internal inflationary policies would inevitably lead in the end to a total monetary collapse.[1]

One of the main effects of the trade and exchange commitments explicitly spelled out in the Rome Treaty would therefore be to accelerate the unavoidable impact which market disciplines would ultimately exercise anyway upon a deficit country's policies. The gradual elimination of tariff, trade, and payments restrictions among members, and the adoption of a common, uniform, commercial policy toward non-members will make it impossible for a deficit country to resort to restrictions as a means to balance its external transactions.[2] Exchange rate readjustments are not entirely ruled out and might even be recommended at times by the Commission to overcome deep-seated malajustments in a country's balance of payments and competitive position. Yet, repeated resort to exchange rate devaluation to offset the incidence of persistently inflationary policies would clearly be incompatible with the Treaty's objectives, and would lead to frequent—even if temporary—distortions in competitive conditions, unacceptable to the country's trading partners. Each Member State is committed to "treat is policy with regard to exchange rates as a matter of common interest" (Article 107) and to "pursue the economic policy necessary to ensure the equilibrium of its overall balance of payments and to maintain confidence in its currency, while ensuring a high level of employment and the stability of the level of prices" (Article 104).

1. I cannot resist the temptation to quote here the following lines from a comedy of Jacques Deval: "Qui croit fuir son destin est seulement attaché à une corde plus longue . . . Mais au bout de la corde, . . . nous faisons tous librement ce qu'il était fatal que nous fassions." Countries will most often adopt "freely" in the end the very policies which internatioanl agreements would have "forced" them to accept more promptly.

2. Although escape clauses allow a country to resort unilaterally to emergency measures in certain cases, the Executive of the Community may impose by means of a qualified majority vote the modification, suspension or elimination of these measures, without the assent of the country concerned.

The final outcome of these Treaty provisions would therefore be to accelerate and strengthen the impact of traditional market forces upon internal policy readjustments for the countries in deficit. The surplus countries, however, are not subject to similiar market pressures and financial limitations. They are always free to offset the internal expansionary impact of their surpluses by "neutralization" or "sterilization" policies. By choosing to do so, and refusing simultaneously to finance their surpluses by capital exports, they may throw upon the deficit countries the whole burden of the internal readjustments necessary to the restoration of equilibrium in the international payments pattern. This "deflationary bias" of the gold standard has often been exaggerated by Keynesian economists, and seems indeed more than compensated today by the "inflationary bias" exercised by pressure groups upon many countries' monetary and fiscal policies. The fact remains, however, that if the harmonization of the member countries' internal policies—*implicitly* required for the observation of the *explicit* clauses of the Treaty relating to restrictions and exchange rates—were left entirely to the disciplines of the market, the latter could only enforce a downward alignment of the more inflationary, or less deflationary, countries upon the less inflationary, or more deflationary, ones. The general pace of expansion of the Community would, in this case, inevitably be set by the least expansionary countries. This is precisely the reason why the sweeping liberalization commitments of the Rome Treaty would have been unacceptable and unnegotiable in the absence of complementary provisions on mutual aid and policy harmonization.

Intergovernmental Cooperation and Policy Harmonization

The broad philosophy underlying the Treaty is that the initial acceptance and later implementation of its liberalization commitments are conditioned by parallel and mutual commitments to coordinate national policies in such a way as to preserve long run equilibrium in the members' balances of payments at high levels of economic activity and employment and stable levels of prices. This philosophy is embedded in various Treaty articles, but its concrete implications are generally left to be worked out, in *ad hoc* fashion, by the institutional organs of the Community.

Article 105 requires the Member States to "institute for this purpose a collaboration between the competent services of their administrative departments and between their central banks. . . .

In order to promote the coordination of the policies of Member States in monetary matters to the full extent necessary to the functioning of the Common Market, a Monetary Committee with consultative status shall hereby be established with the following tasks:

—to keep under review the monetary and financial situation of Member States and of the Community and also the general payments system of Member States and to report regularly thereon to the Council and to the Commission; and

—to formulate opinions, at the request of the Council or of the Commission or on its own initiative, for submission to the said institutions."

The authority and effectiveness of the Monetary Committee are likely to be very much enhanced by its composition, realistically made up of high-ranking officials from both the Ministry of Finance and the Central Bank of each of the participating countries.

Article 108 establishes the procedure to be followed when actual or prospective balance of payments difficulties of a Member State are likely to prejudice the functioning of the Treaty. The Commission must, in such cases, examine without delay the situation of such a State and the action taken by it. "It shall indicate the measures which it recommends to the State concerned to adopt. If the action taken by a Member State and the measures suggested by the Commission do not prove sufficient to overcome the difficulties encountered or threatening, the Commission shall, after consulting the Monetary Committee, recommend to the Council the granting of special assistance and the appropriate methods therefor. . . . The Council, acting by means of a qualified majority vote, shall grant mutual assistance; it shall issue directives or decisions laying down the conditions and particulars thereof. . . ."

Finally, if all these measures prove insufficient, "the Commission shall authorize the State in difficulties to take measures of safeguard of which the Commission shall determine the conditions and particulars." Article 109 authorizes Member States to take such measures "provisionally" if a sudden crisis occurs and if decisions are not reached immediately with respect to mutual assistance.[3] In either case, however, the Council may, by means of qualified majority vote, force the State concerned "to amend, suspend or abolish the measures of safeguard referred to above."

3. Such independent action by a Member, however, can no longer be taken after the end of the transitional period with regard to its trade with non-member countries.

These meetings and consultations may reasonably be expected to exercise in time a growing influence upon the necessary harmonization of member countries' internal policies. The views or recommendations they may express in this respect, however, are in no way binding. Divergencies of national policies may therefore persist up to the point where market forces themselves compel deficit countries to readjust their policies, as the exhaustion or near-exhaustion of their monetary reserves make it impossible for them to finance further balance of payments deficits. Mutual aid credits may postpone this day of reckoning, but such credits can only be granted *"by other Member States, subject to the agreement of the latter."* Cases may therefore arise when mutual aid financing is unanimously recognized as desirable and urgent, but may be delayed unduly, or even blocked, by lack of agreement about the most appropriate sources of such financing. This would be most likely to induce a recourse to the Treaty's escape clauses, unnecessary otherwise, and highly detrimental to all concerned.

A more effective advance planning of mutual assistance financing would seem highly desirable from this point of view alone. It might also help give more weight to the Community's recommendations for policy harmonization and facilitate the gradual acceptance of presumptive criteria, agreed to in advance, and delimiting the respective scopes of independent national action and minimum harmonization requirements in the broad field of monetary and financial policies. Such *ex ante* harmonization would obviously be far preferable to a mere *ex post* harmonization adopted only after considerable damage has been done, and under the pressure of an acute crisis in member countries' balances of payments.

The suggestions outlined below are directed at these two problems. Once again, however, they raise delicate issues on which agreement could not be reached easily without protracted studies and reflexion. Fortunately, the strong reserve and balance of payments position which now characterizes all the Community countries gives them ample time for such consideration.[4] There is little doubt that further agreements will have to be concluded in the future to

4. The monetary reserves of the six countries, as reported in *International Financial Statistics*, have risen from $3.3 billion in 1950 to $10 billion in 1957 and $12.7 in 1958, and their gold and dollar holdings have increased by $2 billion in 1958 alone, from $8.8 billion to $10.8 billion. The six countries together have had current account surpluses with the rest of the world, ranging from $600 million to more than $2 billion a year, in every one of the last six years without exception.

harmonize the monetary institutions of the Community and its international payments machinery with the far-reaching commitments already accepted by it in the field of commercial policy.

A European Community Reserve Fund

The plan previously outlined for a European Clearing House or Reserve Fund would be particularly adaptable to the needs of the European Community. Minimum deposits with a European Community Reserve Fund could provide the easiest and most rational source of financing for mutual credit assistance without endangering in any way the liquidity requirements of the lending countries.

If minimum deposit requirements were to be calculated on this basis alone, a 10 per cent level in relation to gross monetary reserves would endow the Community with an initial working fund of about $1.2 billion, ample to meet any conceivable needs for a considerable time to come. It would be desirable, however, though not essential, to foresee from the beginning gradual increases in this ratio, and this for two reasons. The first is to streamline the relationships which might later be established with a reformed IMF or with the European Clearing House envisaged in the preceding chapters of this book. The Community should ideally participate in either or both of these two institutions as a single unit rather than as a separate collection of individual countries. International credit needs of its members should normally be handled and financed by the Community itself, and involve no transactions with either the IMF or the European Clearing House. The need for such transactions would arise only if the Community Reserve Fund ran short of non-member currencies, or if non-member countries ran short of Community currencies, and if these disequilibria called for legitimate cushioning finance rather than for—or in conjunction with—corrective policies on the part of the countries concerned.

Such a scheme of organization would help decentralize the complex negotiations involved and keep in the hands of the Community itself the leverage necessary to promote the desired harmonization of its members' monetary, financial and economic policies. Deposits with a reformed IMF or with a European Clearing House should thus be maintained by the Community Reserve Fund itself, rather than separately by each of the participating countries. The Community Reserve Fund would, however, have to be increased in such a case beyond the level mentioned above, so as to enable it to maintain the required deposits with the IMF or the European Clearing.

The institution of such a Fund would not entail, of itself, any new and spectacular step toward supranational mechanisms in the monetary field. Its methods of operation could be substantially similar to those suggested above for a wider OEEC Clearing House, except insofar as the Rome Treaty already provides that mutual assistance may be granted by a qualified majority vote of the Council.

Yet, it would be desirable to organize the Fund in such a way as to facilitate some later and gradual shifts of authority and responsibility, in the monetary field, from national institutions to Community institutions.

The experience gained in the initial years of operation of the Monetary Committee in the early detection and readjustment of excessive inflationary or deflationary tendencies in the economy of member countries could, for instance, lead to the definition of presumptive criteria, or danger signals, justifying a stronger intervention of the Community to elicit more rapidly the necessary corrective measures and attempt to forestall *ex ante,* rather than cure *ex post,* foreseeable crises in member countries' balances of payments. It is doubtful indeed whether the Treaty could, in the end, stand the strain of frequently recurring crisis of this sort.

The criteria adopted might be based, for instance, on the amplitude and persistency of changes in employment, economic activity, bank credit, public debt, money supply, prices, monetary reserves, etc. They might initially serve merely to bring automatically into motion a special scrutiny, by the consultative organs of the Community, of the policies followed and of the need for action either by the country itself, or the Community, or both. In the course of time, closer integration might be institutionalized through the adoption of similar criteria as ceilings on independent national decisions. National central banks might, for instance, agree to some presumptive annual ceiling on the growth of their internal credit assets in general, or of some special categories of such assets regarded as particularly open to abuses. Transactions beyond the agreed ceilings might have to be specifically approved by the Commission or the Council, acting upon the recommendations of the Monetary Committee.

The provisions discussed so far all refer to a "downward" harmonization of national "inflationary" policies. An attempt should be made to build up similar safeguards against national "deflationary" policies, affecting unfavourably the balance of payments of other members and slowing down unnecessarily their own rate of expansion. The minimum deposit requirements of members with the Reserve Fund might be raised upon that portion of their monetary reserves which exceeds some pre-agreed benchmark corresponding to "normal" reserve requirements. Deposits widely in excess of such requirements might be subject to funding into medium or long term securities. Provisions might also be made, in such cases, for a levelling down of discount or interest rates in order to encourage desirable credit expansion. Simultaneous increases in abnormally high reserve levels and budgetary surpluses might even ultimately justify directives to the member concerned to either lower taxes, or increase expenditures, etc.

These two issues—*i.e.* the control of "inflationary" or "deflationary" national policies—inevitably raise the problem of defining the desired level of policy harmonization with respect to which these "undesirable" developments can be characterized and measured. Possible divergencies of views among member countries in this respect will necessarily have to be arbitrated here in the light of the development of the balance of payments of the Community as a whole with the rest of the world.

The huge balance of payments surpluses and reserve accumulation of the Community in recent years should make possible the resumption of a relatively fast pace of expansion, together with liberal external trading policies and with a substantial level of capital exports toward the underdeveloped countries, particularly in Europe and its associated monetary areas.

The opposite situation, however, should also be envisaged. Balance of payments deficits with the rest of the world might possibly develop at a later stage as a result of restrictive policies abroad, or of a faster rate of financial expansion in the Community than in the rest of the world. Joint decisions on the part of members would be necessary in this event in order to strengthen their position in international negotiations aimed either at reversing such trends abroad or at obtaining cushioning finance for temporary deficits. They would be even more necessary if the failure of such efforts forced the Community to choose between a slowdown of its own rates of expansion, or a modification of its currencies' parities, or a tightening of its joint tariff, trade and exchange restrictions toward non-members.

Such are the considerations that will have to determine in the end the average expansion pace and monetary policies of the Community, and influence its ability and willingness to grant mutual aid to individual members in difficulty. They are also likely to impose gradually upon its members a more effective machinery for the adoption and implementation of such joint policies than is now contemplated or than is either necessary or possible in the immediate future. A European Community Reserve Fund could become a powerful instrument to bring about the fuller integration of monetary policies that will ultimately be required by the formation of a single trading area, free of internal barriers, and by the conduct of a uniform commercial policy with respect to the external relations of the Community.

Monetary Unification?

An eventual merger of members' national currencies into a single Community currency can only be regarded as highly hypothetical at this stage, and should in any case be envisaged only as the ultimate step of a monetary integration process. It must be emphasized that its desirability as well as its difficulties are essentially political rather than economic. Economically, indeed, a full currency merger would differ very little from a system of free and stable exchange rates among the national currencies of the participating countries. The discipline and limitations which would be imposed upon national policies would be practically identical in both cases. If anything, full currency unity would make this discipline less, rather than more, stringent because it would stimulate an even larger flow of cushioning capital movements to finance temporary disequilibria. The reason for this revolves, in turn, on the one major difference between the two systems. National commitments to exchange rate stability may always be reviewed and revoked, at a later stage, by the national authorities. Even an international agreement might be modified by common consent or broken unilaterally by a country in difficulties. A currency merger, on the other hand, would be very nearly irrevocable and irreversible in practice. This irreversibility constitutes a strong argument against a premature merger. It would probably be unwise to close the door as fully and definitely to exchange rate readjustments until the full impact of the Rome Treaty's commitments to trade liberalization has been absorbed and until experience has demonstrated the feasibility and success of the coordination of internal monetary and financial policies throughout the territory of the Community.

We have already discussed above most of the institutional reforms through which such coordination should gradually be implemented and consolidated in any case, irrespective of the final step toward currency unity. This final step itself, if not undertaken prematurely, would not raise any great difficulties. Three types of measures would help smooth out the transition.

The first would be to authorize and encourage the use of the European unit of account[5] in all international, and even national, capital transactions throughout the Community's territory. This would contribute to the revival of the capital markets still paralyzed or handicapped today by fears of exchange rate instability.

The second step would be the adoption by all member countries of new basic national monetary units identical in value to the European unit of account. Each currency would still retain at this stage its own separate entity and be issued and redeemed by its own national central bank. Since all six currencies would now be equivalent in value, however, they could easily circulate at par throughout the area of the Community and be accepted in payment outside the issuing country's borders. Foreign notes returned by traders to the central bank of the country in which they had been received in payment would be redeemed by the issuing bank, the settlement being immediately effected through respective credits and debits of the clearing accounts of the two central banks concerned with the Community Reserve Fund. This intercirculation privilege would bear a close resemblance to the old Latin Union which similarly ensured for many years before the first world war the intercirculation of silver coins whose metallic value diverged substantially from their nominal value.[6] Any subsequent exchange rate readjustment would inevitably deprive the currency concerned from the intercircu-

5. See above p. 125 and footnote.

6. This historical precedent would suggest the adoption of national units—and of a European unit—equal to one fifth of the present gold content of the U.S. dollar. This would restore the traditional relationship of most continental currencies to the U.S. dollar, such as was preserved throughout the nineteenth century on the basis of the famous "germinal" franc. If, as now appears likely, the currencies of the Six are finally stabilized on the basis of their present exchange rates, the proposed new unit would be exchanged practically at par for the new "heavy" French franc, at one to ten for Belgian and Luxemburgese francs, at one to 125 for Italian lire, at one to 0.84 for German marks, and at one to 0.76 for Dutch guilders.

lation privilege. This would act as a powerful deterrent to such readjustments and reinforce exchange rate stability as an important goal of economic policy for the six countries of the Community.

The final stage of monetary unification would then merely require the nominal transfer of the outstanding assets and liabilities of the national central banks to a joint European Monetary Authority. This need not involve any radical alteration in the central banking structure of the Community if all the institutional prerequisites mentioned earlier in this paper had been previously fulfilled. The European Monetary Authority could be organized on a largely decentralized basis, retaining the individuality of the present national central banks as operating institutions for the system, just as the twelve Federal Reserve Banks of the United States carry out in practice all the transactions of the Federal Reserve System. Each national bank would continue to manage its own monetary and credit operations within agreed statutory limits, and under the general supervision of the European Monetary Authority. The statutory rules to be adopted would probably include the setting up of national credit ceilings, to be exceeded only with the approval of the European Monetary Authority, of minimum reserve ratios, and other regulatory techniques inspired from present central banking legislations in the Community and abroad, and from the experience acquired by the European Community Reserve Fund and the Monetary Committee.

An equitable distribution of the burden associated with the maintenance of adequate reserve levels of gold and foreign exchange by the Community as a whole would probably require that each national bank observe some minimum prescriptions with regard to such holdings. These prescriptions might be met at the outset through the negotiation of initial, interest-bearing, stabilization loans, at long or medium term, by the low reserve countries, either abroad or with the high reserve countries. Later reserve deficiencies could be met by special advances or investments of the Community Reserve Fund, or by open market transactions in approved securities among the participating banks.

The reader will note that many of the substantive aspects of such a reform would already have been put into operation by the Monetary Committee and the Community Reserve Fund, if the institutional prerequisites to monetary unification had been previously fulfilled. This confirms the view, expressed above, that the real significance of monetary unification is political far more than economic. The fundamental problems which should be raised before such a spectacular decision becomes either desirable or possible are:

1) The acceptance of such an irreversible step toward monetary unification as a political goal, dramatizing and consolidating the will of the Six to achieve a full merger of their national economic sovereignties;

2) The development of a sufficient degree of confidence in the feasibility of this objective, on the basis of protracted experience with a *de facto* harmonization of national policies, the success of which would have been demonstrated by the full observance of the members' liberalization commitments together with the maintenance of exchange rate stability among their separate currencies;

3) The institutionalization of the anonymous market "discipline" involved in this *de facto* harmonization, through administrative rules and procedures, agreed to among members, particularly with reference to the monetization of internal credits by the banking system.

Monetary unification must be conceived therefore as the crowning step of the six countries' integration policies. It should guide and inspire such policies, but its premature adoption would involve enormous risks of setbacks which might be fatal to its consolidation and ultimate success.

Summary and Conclusions

1. The European convertibility decisions of December 1958 mark an important step forward on the long road from the international monetary chaos of the last decades toward a new international monetary order. Of and by themselves, however, they merely return the world to the unorganized and nationalistic gold exchange standard of the late 1920's. The utter irrationality of such a system, and its extreme vulnerability to unfavorable developments in the few "key currency" countries on which it rests, were unanimously denounced by all economists at that time, and the wisdom of these warnings was quickly and catastrophically demonstrated by the collapse of the gold exchange standard a few years later, in 1931.

Inadequate gold supplies are supplemented, in such a system, by a growing accumulation of *national* key currencies as *international* reserves. Such accumulation inevitably centers on the "safest" currencies of major creditor countries and results in "unrequited" capital imports by them. The very countries that should lend to the others are thus unwittingly borrowing short term capital from them. These capital movements do not, by themselves, relieve the gold shortage, but merely disguise it as a shortage of the key currencies in question. In order to contribute to the needed expansion of world liquidity, they must stimulate additional matching capital exports by the key currency countries, or a contraction of their surpluses on current account. Either of these reactions, however, cannot but lead to a progressive and persistent deterioration in their net reserve position up to the point where their currency no longer appears as the "safest" for reserve investment by other countries. The consequent slowdown, cessation, or reversal of the accumulation of key currencies as world reserves then brings back to the fore the underlying gold shortage problem and imposes at the same time difficult balance of payments readjustments upon the center countries of the system. Internal deflation, currency devaluation, or trade and exchange restrictions will be the main choices open to them, will tend to spread from the center countries to the rest of the world, and may be further aggravated by speculative capital movements culminating in a financial panic à la 1931, or/and a relapse into bilateralism.

The recent deterioration of the United States balance of payments, the persistent weakness of the dollar on the exchange markets, the huge gold losses of 1958 and the re-awakening of protectionist forces in the Administration and the Congress would fit this analysis. Heed should be paid to these ominous portents of future trouble before the crisis is upon us.

2. The internationalization of foreign exchange reserves under the aegis of the International Monetary Fund has been advocated above as the most logical solution of this problem. It would facilitate the adjustment of the Fund's lending operations to the legitimate liquidity requirements of an expanding world economy, and help stabilize the world monetary system against the vicissitudes of national monetary management in the present key currency countries. Concrete measures have been proposed to safeguard such a truly *international* gold exchange standard against the inflationary bias which caused the rejection, fifteen years ago, of the broadly similar proposals of John Maynard Keynes.

3. A workable and viable system of international monetary convertibility will also depend, tomorrow as it did yesterday, on an ample provision of cushioning capital to finance temporary disequilibria, and on the correlative acceptance and implementation of a coordination of internal financial policies sufficient to preserve long run equilibrium in each country's overall balance of payments. The internationalization of foreign exchange reserves would help provide this financing and give the International Monetary Fund the necessary leverage to promote such harmonization.

4. Convertibility cannot be meaningfully defined for policy purposes, except as a relative concept whose ultimate culmination would imply the total surrender of national sovereignty by member countries over all forms of trade and payments restrictions, and even over exchange rates. Such surrenders are utterly inconceivable today in favor of a mere nineteenth century *laissez faire,* unconcerned with national levels of employment and economic activity. The negotiation and implementation of negative convertibility commitments are inseparable from the parallel negotiation and implementation of positive integration commitments among the countries concerned. National policy instruments cannot be thrown away. They can only

be traded against international, or supranational policy instruments adequate to serve the broad objectives of economic policy in the modern world.

5. The political, administrative, and psychological obstacles to full integration dictate a flexible approach to the problem of convertibility itself. Every opportunity for negotiable and workable agreements should be exploited as fully as possible, both on the worldwide level and on the regional levels. The potentialities of these latter forms of integration have been convincingly demonstrated by the success of OEEC cooperation since the war, by the recent setting up of the European Economic Community, by the continuing endeavors to establish a European Free Trade Area or Economic Association, and by similar proposals for regional integration in other parts of the world.[1] Closer regional agreements of this type can usefully supplement and support the looser agreements attainable on a world-wide level, and pave the way, under favorable conditions, for a complete merger of economic sovereignty among the participating countries. The last two chapters have summarized the main features of the present European Monetary Agreement and suggested that it be strengthened and consolidated into a European Clearing Union or Reserve Fund, in order to provide a viable monetary and payments framework for the extensive trade commitments of a European Economic Association and of the European Economic Community. Such a Fund might, in the latter context, evolve gradually into a Federal Monetary Authority and provide the institutional machinery required for an eventual merger of the six countries' national currencies.

1. The feasibility of such integration agreements outside Western Europe, and the adjustment of their aims and techniques to very different economic conditions, could not be discussed in this study. The reader may find a few introductory remarks to the problem in a paper of mine on "Latin America in World Trade and Payments" reproduced in the *Proceedings of the Fifth Meeting of Technicians of Central Banks of the American Continent,* Bogota (Colombia), 1957.

Postscript

To Bring Up to Date an Unfinished Story

1. Initial Reactions, Official and Other

The Postscript to the first edition of this book quoted at some length the "initial reactions, official and other" which greeted its initial appearance in article form in the March and June 1959 issues of the *Banca Nazionale del Lavoro Quarterly Review*.

In brief:

1. The reaction of a group of economists and central bankers, at a meeting of the International Economic Association in Elsinore, in September 1959, was summarized as follows by Leonard Silk in *Business Week*:

> Triffin's warning that the real danger ahead is not inflation but deflation resulting from a liquidity crisis got a mixed reception. Outside the meetings, some economists voiced strong support for his views. Others—particularly the central bankers —were more cautious, saying it was impossible at this stage to pass judgment on his diagnosis or his solution. All pledged careful study of the question.
>
> There was little inclination, at any rate, to scoff at Triffin's warning, for his prestige as an economist and monetary expert is high. He fathered the European Payments Union and, more than any other man, negotiated it into existence.

2. In Britain, the Radcliffe Committee on the Working of the Monetary System unanimously endorsed, as a long-term objective, proposals "for transformation of the International Monetary Fund, along the lines originally proposed by the United Kingdom [in the Keynes plan], into an international central bank, with its own unit of account, free to accept deposit liabilities or extend overdraft facilities to the central banks of member countries."

The Committee was considerably cooler, on the other hand, about the proposals for a compulsory conversion of outstanding reserves in national currencies—primarily sterling and dollar balances—into Fund deposits. "An arrangement of this kind, requiring international agreement, would be extremely difficult to negotiate and does not appear to us likely to be of immediate and substantial assistance to sterling; it might, indeed, oblige the United Kingdom to discharge her external liabilities more quickly than would otherwise be necessary." *

3. On the continent, Jean Monnet's Action Committee for the United States of Europe adopted unanimously in November 1959 a joint declaration, the last section of which specifically endorsed the proposals presented on pages 138–141 above:

> The Action Committee for the United States of Europe would like to request the Council of Ministers of Finance of the six countries to include on the agenda of one of their next meetings, and to examine as a matter of urgency, the following questions of European financial policy, which in the Committee's opinion are of the greatest importance. . . .
>
> .   .   .
>
> 3.—setting up a European Reserve Fund which would centralise at least a part of the six countries' monetary reserves and in time of need enable the mutual aid procedures provided for in the Treaty to be put into operation, thus safeguarding the currencies of our countries.

Paradoxically enough, but very encouragingly, the warmest applause to this declaration came from . . . England. The London *Economist* commented on December 12, 1959 (pages 1083–1084):

> Last month's meeting of M. Monnet's committee produced much that was familiar . . . But one section of the resolution that was passed went beyond the ordinary . . .
>
> There need be no doubt of the value of such a project if it were ever realised. To make a common policy really effective and expansionist, an economic union needs some such device. An article on page 702 of *The Economist* of November 21st suggested that any massive increase in European capital exports to the undeveloped world would require a major expansion of world liquidity. In the past the International Monetary Fund has lacked the political authority to carry out such big and long-term transfers of resources. Here at last is a part answer—a scheme for enhancing liquidity on a European basis within a system which has political teeth.

* Committee on the Working of the Monetary System, *Report* (London, Her Majesty's Stationery Office, 1959), pp. 247–248.

As an outsider Britain might well see such a project as a competitive threat to the status of sterling. Certainly, if Britain were in the scheme, sterling would stand to gain greatly from it. But the scheme has a chance of success just because it involves a greater pooling of sovereignty than Britain has yet been prepared to accept.

4. On October 9, 1959, I was invited by Senator Paul H. Douglas to present my views to the Joint Economic Committee of Congress. The debate that followed my testimony, on October 28, seemed to me to give a strong indication that Congress might be more receptive to bold, forward-looking proposals for international monetary reform than had been generally believed by timid Administration officials. The very real political difficulties involved stemmed far more from the reluctance of our political leaders to lead than from the refusal of Congress and political opinion to accept such leadership.

After obtaining unanimous concurrence from his Committee, Senator Paul H. Douglas transmitted my statement and a transcript of the hearings to the President, the Secretary of the Treasury, the Chairman of the Board of Governors of the Federal Reserve System, the Managing Director of the International Monetary Fund, and the respective Chairmen of the House and Senate Banking and Currency Committees, the Senate Finance Committee and Foreign Relations Committee, and the House Foreign Affairs Committee and Ways and Means Committee.

His covering letter to the President said:

Dear Mr. President:

The Joint Economic Committee wishes to bring to your attention a most interesting and stimulating suggestion presented to the committee in its public hearings Wednesday afternoon by Professor Robert Triffin, of Yale University. Professor Triffin, an internationally known authority on international monetary problems, has suggested the revision of the International Monetary Fund or the creation of a new organization to replace the present one which, if successful, would solve problems both of the United States and of other countries maintaining liquidity reserves required by international financial transactions. The committee, of course, has not had an opportunity to consider

Professor Triffin's suggestion and as a committee is not pre-pared to endorse his recommendations. We do believe, however, that his suggestion is of sufficient merit and originality that it deserves the most serious and intensive study on the part of responsible officials.

In view of these facts, the committee is taking the somewhat unusual course of transmitting to you for your consideration and, we hope, your comments, a copy of Mr. Triffin's statement and the transcript of the day's hearing.

Faithfully yours,
PAUL H. DOUGLAS, Chairman.

5. The outgoing Administration, however, was in no mood to tackle such a problem during its last months in office. I had no knowledge at the time of the answers given to Senator Douglas, but could guess that they were either evasive, or downright negative.*

A blank page in my book regrettably seemed to me the most ade-quate way to convey to the reader the full flavor of the Administra-tion's reaction to my diagnosis and proposals.

---

* Confirmation of this guess is now available in the documents published in the December 8, 1960, *Hearings* of the Joint Economic Committee on the *Current Economic Situation and Short-Run Outlook*, Washington, 1961, pp. 171 ff.

2. The September 1960 Meeting of the International Monetary Fund

At the annual meeting of the Board of Governors of the International Monetary Fund in Washington, at the end of September 1960, Secretary of the Treasury Anderson and several other speakers referred to the recent "discussion of the way in which the international financial system is functioning" and to the "suggestions . . . for changes which might be made in that system," but only to conclude that:

> the international system has continued to function efficiently in financing trade and providing increased movement of short-term funds among a widening group of convertible currencies . . . This emerging convertibility, together with the renewed vigor of commercial banking institutions in the international field and the strengthening of the Fund resources, has contributed to the flexible and smooth operation of the system . . . We are not confronted with any immediate need to consider changes in the system as a whole or in the International Monetary Fund.

This bland optimism, however, was not shared by all, and particularly not by the British Chancellor of the Exchequer. He called attention to the "disquieting features" of the international payments situation and questioned

> the method of operation of the Fund. Is there a danger of these operations exacerbating the problem of imbalance because of the tendency for members in short-term difficulties to take drawings from the Fund in only a limited range of currencies? . . . The history of past drawings from the Fund shows that these have been concentrated to a very large extent on the U.S. dollar . . . Undue concentration on the reserve currencies might have unfortunate consequences in the future* . . . I am sure that this subject is not new to the Fund, but I think it would bear further study now that we can look at it not as something

---

* Compare my remarks on the same subject, at the bottom of p. 12 and top of p. 13, and on pp. 116–117.

imminent, but as something which could become real at some future date and which in common prudence we ought to provide for. We should be glad to cooperate in such a study and should be ready to make some practical suggestions.

Governor Cuaderno of the Philippines was even blunter in quoting my fears that "the new experiment in convertibility . . . faces the same two threats that wrecked a similar experiment some thirty years ago" and in expressing his belief that "Dr. Triffin's warning of a possible crisis in the world's monetary reserves and the various measures that have been suggested to arrest it should be looked into by the Fund authorities."

3. The Break in the London Gold Market

The delegates to the IMF meeting had hardly returned home when the official optimism that had suffused that gathering was badly shattered by the sudden flare-up of gold prices in the London market. On October 20, the dollar price of gold, which was $35.24 an ounce at the beginning of the week and until recently had not exceeded $35.15, jumped precipitously, if briefly, beyond $40 an ounce to settle back later in the day around $38 an ounce, i.e. 8 to 9 per cent higher than would correspond to the official par value of the dollar.

The most extraordinary comment elicited by this event was undoubtedly that of our Treasury spokesman, as quoted in an Associated Press dispatch that evening: "We are watching it closely. We are wondering just what has happened. . . ."

What had happened, of course, was that an abrupt cessation of the previously large sales of Russian gold to the West had aggravated other sources of strain on the market, forcing the Bank of England to intervene on an increasing scale in order to keep the market orderly. Some of our Treasury people, however, still seemed to stick to the specious view that the price paid for gold by private speculators was of no interest to us and that scarce gold reserves should be held exclusively by the monetary authorities rather than dispersed into private hands. Press dispatches suggest that doubts may have been raised unofficially by such people, during the September IMF gatherings, as to whether or not gold sales by the Bank of England on the free market fell within the scope of the "legitimate monetary purposes" conditioning central banks' access to our own Treasury gold.

A trip of a Bank of England Director to Washington was hurriedly arranged to dispel these doubts, but all the harm that had been so foolishly done could not be so quickly undone. The gold scare had attracted new speculators to the market, including many Americans who had never dreamed before of buying gold. Larger sales of American gold by the Bank of England brought down the price in the following weeks, but stopped short of what would have been needed to restore it to parity. Slight, but continuing, premiums persisted well into 1961, and kept alive speculative uncertainties as to the future course of the dollar-gold rate.

United States gold losses jumped from $50 million in the first quarter of 1960 to $94 million in the second quarter, $638 million in the third quarter and—in spite of a $300 million gold loan by the IMF—to $958 million in the fourth quarter, i.e. an annual rate of nearly $4 billion—and of more than $5 billion if we discount the impact of this IMF transaction.

4. The Evolution of the U.S. Balance of Payments

A wave of panic swept over Washington officialdom. A number of measures were hastily concocted to reduce military spending abroad and poor Mr. Anderson was hurriedly dispatched on a wild goose chase to Germany to beg the Germans to pay for our troops stationed on German soil.

This belated concern spelled at least the end of the incomprehensible complacency with which we had observed our persistent balance of payments deficits on over-all account during the last decade, and their sudden spurt to a rate of $3 billion to $4 billion a year in 1958, 1959, and 1960. Yet, the measures adopted reflected a totally unwarranted sense of panic. Most of all, they centered almost exclusively on a facet of the problem which was already well on its way to a solution, but they failed to recognize the real threat which confronted us, and the rest of the free world, in the closing months of 1960.

Table 20 shows that the alarming deterioration of our current account balance in 1958 and 1959—from an average surplus of $2.1 billion over the years 1952–1957 to a deficit of $0.9 billion in 1959—had been sharply reversed already by the fall of 1960. Our 1959 *deficit* of $0.9 billion had been replaced by record *surpluses* running at an annual rate of $2.4 billion for the first nine months of 1960, and $3.4 billion in the third quarter. This was amply sufficient to finance near record levels of $2.5 to $3.0 billion a year of government capital exports and economic aid. Our surpluses were undoubtedly receiving a somewhat precarious boost from the timing of huge cotton and jet aircraft sales, and especially from the coincidence of booming export markets in Europe and Japan with an incipient recession here. Yet, a $3 billion to $4 billion improvement in our current balance in such a short space of time was highly encouraging, and delayed upward adjustments of European wages and expenditures to the spectacular growth of Europe's production and exports were likely to improve further our own competitive position in world markets.

The real trouble lay elsewhere. It stemmed from a drastic increase in net exports of private capital—American and foreign—from this country. Exclusive of so-called liquid dollar balances recorded as

TABLE 20
Balance of Payments of the United States, 1952–1960
(*Annual rates, seasonally adjusted, in billions of dollars*)

| | Years | | | | | Change from 1959 to | |
| | | | | 1960 | | First nine months of 1960 | Third quarter of 1960 |
	1952–57	1958	1959	First nine months	Third quarter		
1. Current Account	+2.1	+1.5	−0.9	+2.4	+3.4	+3.3	+4.3
2. U.S. Government Aid and Capital Exports (−)	−2.2	−2.6	−2.0	−2.6	−3.0	−0.6	−1.0
3. *Subtotal* (1 + 2)	*−0.1*	*−1.1*	*−2.9*	*−0.2*	*+0.5*	*+2.7*	*+3.4*
4. Other U.S. and Foreign Capital	−1.0	−2.4	−0.8	−3.0	−4.6	−2.2	−3.8
5. *Total* (3 + 4) = Gold and Dollar Settlements	**−1.1**	**−3.5**	**−3.8**	**−3.2**	**−4.1**	**+0.6**	**−0.3**

Notes:
1. The current account estimates under (1) include U.S. military expenditures abroad, private remittances, and pensions and other transfers.
2. Items 2 and 5 exclude, in 1959, transactions arising from the U.S. subscription to the increase in the capital of the International Monetary Fund.
3. Item 4 includes "Errors and Omissions." The deterioration in the capital accounts summarized under this item does not reveal, however, the further deterioration arising from the sales of private dollar balances to official holders, which began in the third quarter of 1960 and reached a peak during the following months.
4. Small discrepancies in additions are due to rounding.

Source: Survey of Current Business, December 1960.

"settlements" rather than as "capital exports," this outflow had risen from $0.8 billion in 1959 to an annual rate of more than $4½ billion in the third quarter of 1960. Thus it is that a record rate in our "over-all" deficit ($4.1 billion) coincided with a near record rate in our current account *surplus* ($3.4 billion).

Most of this reflected the shift of short-term funds, highly responsive to differential interest rates between major financial centers and to speculative rumors regarding the future course of exchange rates. High interest rates were maintained in Germany in the face of huge balance of payments surpluses, and influenced the course of interest rates in other European places, particularly London. This coincided with low interest rates here—under the influence of a recession in domestic economic activity—in the face of huge balance of payments deficits. The well-known weaknesses of the gold exchange standard, responsible for its downfall in 1931, were once more in evidence, less than two years after the much-heralded restoration of the system in December 1958.

The vulnerability imparted by the gold exchange standard to the major key currency supporting its operation is all the greater today in view of the enormous size of the dollar balances accumulated by foreigners over the last decade. These rose from $8.2 billion in 1949 to $23.7 billion in 1960. Particularly disquieting was the fact that privately-held dollar balances had stopped increasing after June, the whole of the later increases being absorbed by central banks—with a growing reluctance—and by the International Monetary Fund (see Table 21). Private bank balances declined indeed by $600 million in the last quarter of 1960.

TABLE 21

International Liquidity Position of the United States, 1938–1960

(*in billions of dollars*)

End of	1938	1949	1952	1957	1958	1959	1960 June	Sept.	Oct.	Dec.
I. *Gross Assets*	15.2	28.1	27.1	27.8	25.9	26.3	26.3	26.0	25.9	25.5
1. Gold	14.6	24.6	23.3	22.9	20.6	19.5	19.4	18.7	18.4	17.8
2. Foreign Exchange	0.6	0.8	1.0	2.2	2.5	2.6	2.8	3.1	3.3	3.6
3. IMF Quota	—	2.8	2.8	2.8	2.8	4.1	4.1	4.1	4.1	4.1
II. *Gross Liabilities*	2.2	8.2	11.7	16.6	17.6	21.6	22.8	23.4	23.5	23.7
1. Foreign Countries:	2.2	6.4	9.9	14.9	15.6	17.7	18.7	19.1	19.2	18.8
a) Official		3.1	4.9	7.9	8.7	9.1	9.6	10.1	10.3	10.4
b) Banks		} 2.9	{ 2.4	3.5	3.5	4.7	5.3	5.3	5.2	4.7
c) Other			{ 1.7	2.2	2.4	2.4	2.3	2.2	2.3	2.3
d) Bonds and Notes		0.4	0.9	1.2	1.0	1.5	1.6	1.5	1.4	1.4
2. International	—	1.8	1.9	1.7	2.0	3.8	4.1	4.2	4.4	4.8
III. *Net Assets*										
1. I minus II	13.0	19.9	15.3	11.2	8.2	4.7	3.5	2.6	2.3	1.8
2. I,1 minus II,1	12.4	18.2	13.4	8.0	5.0	1.8	0.7	−0.4	−0.8	−1.0

Source: Computed from *Federal Reserve Bulletin* data and estimates.

We ran no danger of becoming insolvent. The growth of our long-term and private assets abroad—particularly direct investments—far outran the deterioration in our net reserve position. But the latter indicated a continuous and dangerous weakening in our liquidity position (see Table 21, lines III, 1 and 2).

5. The Twilight of the Gold Exchange Standard

The vulnerability of the key currencies to the functioning of the gold exchange standard is paralleled by a reverse vulnerability of the gold exchange standard itself to the fate of the key currencies upon

TABLE 22
World Monetary Gold and Dollar Holdings, 1949–1960
(*in billions of dollars*)

	End of					Change	
	1949	*1952*	*1957*	*1959*	*Sept. 1960*	*1949– Sept. 1960*	*1957– Sept. 1960*
I. *Monetary Gold*	34.7	35.8	38.8	40.2	40.7	+6.0	+1.9
A. International Institutions	1.5	1.7	1.2	2.4	2.6	+1.1	+1.4
B. United States	24.6	23.3	22.9	19.5	18.7	−5.8	−4.1
C. Rest of World	8.6	10.9	14.8	18.3	19.4	+10.8	+4.6
II. *Foreign Dollar Holdings*	8.2	11.7	16.6	21.6	23.4	+15.2	+6.8
A. International Institutions	1.8	1.9	1.7	3.8	4.2	+2.4	+2.5
B. Rest of World	6.4	9.9	14.9	17.7	19.1	+12.7	+4.3
III. *Total*							
Gross (I + II)	42.9	47.6	55.4	61.7	64.1	+21.2	+8.6
Net (= I)	34.7	35.8	38.8	40.2	40.7	+6.0	+1.9
A. International Institutions (IA + IIA)	3.3	3.5	2.9	6.2	6.8	+3.5	+3.9
B. United States (IB − II)	16.3	11.5	6.3	−2.0	−4.7	−21.0	−10.9
C. Rest of World (IC + IIB)	15.0	20.8	29.6	36.0	38.5	+23.5	+8.9

Source: Computed from *Federal Reserve Bulletin* data and estimates. Note that a large portion of increases of monetary gold in recent years has been derived from USSR sales in Western markets, rather than from current gold production in the West.

which it rests. The extent and growth of this interdependence may be gauged from Tables 22, 23, and especially 24.*

* Minor discrepancies between some estimates in these tables and comparable ones in previous tables in this volume are due to the constant process of revision which

TABLE 23

World Monetary Reserves, 1913–1959

	1913	1928	1933	1938	1949	1959
I. *In Per cent of Imports*						
A. *World*	**37**	**45**	**110**	**118**	**79**	**56**
1. Gold	35	34	101	111	58	38
2. Foreign Exchange	2	11	9	8	21	18
B. *World outside U.S. and U.K.*	**35**	**44**	**93**	**62**	**48**	**48**
1. Gold	32	29	81	51	21	23
2. Foreign Exchange	3	16	12	11	27	24
a) Dollar	1	3	1	3	7	12
b) Sterling and Other	3	13	11	8	20	12
II. *In Per cent of Total Reserves*						
A. *World*	100	100	100	100	100	100
1. Gold	94	77	92	94	74	67
2. Foreign Exchange	6	23	8	6	26	33
B. *World outside U.K. and U.S.*	100	100	100	100	100	100
1. Gold	91	64	87	83	43	49
2. Foreign Exchange	9	36	13	17	57	51
a) Dollar	2	7	1	5	15	25
b) Sterling and Other	7	29	12	12	42	26

Source: These estimates are derived from Federal Reserve and IMF publications. They exclude the Eastern bloc countries throughout and are subject to a larger margin of error for the years before 1938. Reserve figures include gold coin in circulation in 1913 and 1928, IMF gold (but not local currency assets) and BIS, EPU, and European Fund reserves.

Of the $27 billion increase in foreign countries' and international institutions' gold reserves and foreign dollar holdings—public and private—from the end of 1949 to the end of September 1960, only $6 billion were derived from new gold production and Russian gold sales in Western markets. The overwhelming bulk of the increase

gold and reserve statistics are undergoing at the hands of the IMF and of the Federal Reserve. New estimates on the structure of sterling balances, for instance, have become available only recently. A number of new countries have also gradually been added in the reporting of reserve statistics, while on the other hand previous estimates have been deflated to exclude double counting of BIS gold and foreign exchange holdings and of countries' deposits at the BIS.

sprang from our own gold losses ($5.8 billion) and increases in short-term liabilities abroad ($15.2 billion).† Can anyone imagine that the use of the dollar as a key currency for reserve accumulation by other countries could survive much longer a continuation of such a weakening—even at a reduced rate—in our net reserve position?

Tables 23 and 24 analyze the structure of world reserves in general, including official sterling as well as dollar balances, but excluding private holdings of these currencies.

The salient facts brought out by Table 23 are:

1. The lowering of the ratio of reserves, and particularly gold reserves, to imports since 1933 (see lines I A, I A1, I B and I B1). While some of these ratios are still higher than in 1913 or 1928, one should not forget that the fears universally expressed around the latter year about the consequences of a gold scarcity relieved by an exaggerated dependence on an unorganized and nationalistic gold exchange standard were dramatically confirmed by the collapse of the world monetary system in 1931.

2. The spectacular shift in the structure of reserves outside the key currency countries from 91 per cent gold and 9 per cent foreign exchange in 1913 to 49 per cent gold and 51 per cent foreign exchange in 1959. Admittedly, the relative share of foreign exchange reserves in the total was even higher in 1949, but sterling—which then made up the bulk of these foreign exchange holdings—was then, and remained for years, an inconvertible currency.

Table 24 is even more telling. It brings out the utter dependence of the present world monetary system on totally erratic and haphazard sources of reserve supply in an expanding world economy (see particularly columns 1 and 6):

1. Gold production in the West (line I A1) has provided less than half of the increases in world reserves in the last half-century, and barely a third in the last ten years. Even this source of supply might be seriously disturbed tomorrow by the threatening eruption of racial warfare in the major gold-producing country, South Africa.

2. The withdrawal of gold coin from circulation, and the 1933 devaluation of the dollar contributed major shares of reserve increases in the 1920's and 1930's (see lines I A2 and 3). The first of these two sources may, of course, be regarded as exhausted for practical purposes, while wilful recourse to the second would be an act

† See lines III A and C, I, I B and II in penultimate column of Table 22.

TABLE 24

Sources of Increases in World Reserves, 1914–1959

(in per cent of total increases)

	1914–59	1914–28	1929–33	1934–38	1939–49	1950–59	1958–59
I. World							
A. *Monetary gold*	**66**	**68**	**131**	**80**	**47**	**43**	**91**
1. Production	43	38	12	90	46	34	59
2. Coin Withdrawal	6	30	10	—	—	—	—
3. Dollar Devaluation	15	—	109	—	—	—	—
4. USSR Sales	2	—	—	−1	1	9	32
B. *Foreign Exchange*	**34**	**32**	**−31**	**11**	**53**	**57**	**9**
1. Dollar	17	6	−7	5	13	50	70
2. Sterling and Other	17	26	−24	5	41	7	−60
II. World outside the United States							
A. *U.S. Transactions*						65	92
1. U.S. Gold Losses						29	67
2. Increases in Official Dollar Balances						36	24
B. *Other Sources*						35	8
1. Foreign Gold						30	26
a) Production						24	17
b) USSR Sales						6	9
2. Other Transactions						5	−18
a) Official Sterling Balances							−2
b) Other Reserve Balances							−16

Source: See Table 23. The breakdown between gold and foreign exchange—particularly reserve balances other than sterling and dollars—is distorted in 1959 by the exclusion from reserve calculations of the EPU balances, following their consolidation upon the expiration of the EPU Agreement.

of sheer folly, for reasons amply discussed on pages 79-82 of this book.

3. USSR sales to the West (line I A4) have become a major source of reserve increases in recent years. Their abrupt cessation in recent months certainly played a part in the London gold crisis of October 1960. Does anyone wish to abandon forever such an important role in the regulation of monetary gold supplies in the West to the whims or policies of Mr. Khrushchev?

4. The persistent growth of our short-term indebtedness to foreign central banks has contributed half of the world reserve increases of the last decade, and as much as 70 per cent in 1958–1959 (line I B1). World reserves outside the United States have been fed—to the extent of two-thirds over the last ten years, and 92 per cent in 1958–1959—by our gold losses and the increase in our short-term liabilities to foreign central banks and international institutions (line II A). The reasons why this process cannot continue indefinitely are now clear to everybody. But can anyone, regardless of his views as to precise requirements for reserve increases in an expanding world economy, contemplate with equanimity the long-run consequences of the drying up of two-thirds of the sources of reserve increases in the 1950's?

6. The Prospects for Action

Such are the arguments I have repeatedly used over the last year, with academic or governmental experts as well as before lay audiences, in an effort to stimulate a long-overdue reform of an outworn international monetary system which has functioned only rarely and fitfully since the collapse of the old gold standard during the First World War.

The forces of inertia and the fears of a jump into the unfamiliar are far from vanquished. Yet, the signs of an active interest in the problem have been multiplying in recent months.

In Latin America. At the Sixth Meeting of Technicians of Central Banks of the American Continent, held in Guatemala in November 1960, the response of all the Latin American delegates was highly encouraging. Several speakers urged their colleagues, without any dissent from any of them, to study the problem and argue the case with their respective governments, so as to elicit joint action and support by all the Latin American countries in future discussions and international negotiations.

The representatives of Central America who attended the meeting unanimously endorsed my suggestion for the creation of a Central American Payments Union modelled upon the project for a European Community Reserve Fund outlined on pages 138-141 of this volume. Two weeks later, a special provision to this effect was inserted by their Finance Ministers in the Agreement for the Establishment of a Central American Bank for Economic Integration.

In Europe. European central bankers were at first, and may still be, highly skeptical. Two conferences of mine, last summer, at the Sociétés d'Economie Politique of France and Belgium* did, however, attract considerable attention. During a flying visit to Europe at the end of December 1960, I had a further opportunity to discuss privately, with a number of interested friends, some of the major

* "Le Crépuscule de l'Etalon de Change-Or," published in the *Comptes Rendus de la Société Royale d'Economie Politique de Belgique*, No. 272, Brussels, June 1960, and in *Problèmes Economiques*, No. 665, Paris, September 1960. See also "Integration Economique Européenne et Politique Monétaire" in a special number of the *Revue d'Economie Politique* entitled "La Restauration des Monnaies Européennes," Paris, 1960.

issues involved. I found responsible officials highly perturbed about the dangers then facing the dollar, but determined to cooperate fully with us to solve what they regarded as a common problem of the West. The dollar crisis, they felt, was primarily a symptom of deeper structural faults in the international monetary system. What was needed was not a salvage operation centering on the dollar alone, but a consolidation and revitalization of the international monetary system itself. No country, however, was inclined to take concrete initiatives in the matter, and all were hoping for some sign of leadership from the key currency countries, and particularly from the United States.

The following article of Edwin L. Dale, Jr., in the January 18th, 1961 issue of the *New York Times* seems to me to reflect with great accuracy and acumen the attitude of the European monetary officials at the time.

MONETARY CHANGE STUDIED IN EUROPE

Common Market Countries Consider Alternatives to Present World System

By EDWIN L. DALE, JR.
Special to The New York Times

PARIS, Jan. 17—The finance ministries and central banks of six European countries have begun a study to see whether the present world monetary system, which is based mainly on gold, dollars and pounds sterling, ought to be changed.

This marks a major step. There has been an almost instinctive opposition, among central banks in particular, to proposals for changing the world's monetary arrangement.

The new study does not imply a conclusion that the system should be changed, officials stressed. But they agreed that the study itself was an indication of some alteration of position.

Almost as important as the study itself was the fact that the six governments were willing to announce it publicly. The occasion was a news conference following a week-end meeting at the Hague, the Netherlands, of the finance ministers and central banks chiefs of the six members of the European Economic Community or Common Market—France, West Germany, Italy, Belgium, the Netherlands and Luxembourg.

Dollar Troubles Noted

The current troubles of the dollar and the recent big gold loss of the United States are clearly the prime movers behind the study. But various experts have argued that, even without a dollar crisis, a change in the system will soon be necessary.

Any change would have to have the agreement of all the major trading nations, including, above all, the United States. Under the Eisenhower Administration the United States Treasury was always unsympathetic to proposals for a change, partly on the ground that an effort to change the system would appear to be a sign of weakness.

However, there have been hints that the incoming Democratic Administration might take a different attitude. If there should emerge a common will to seek a new arrangement, the probability is that some sort of world monetary conference would be the vehicle for working it out.

The most discussed proposal for a change has come from Prof. Robert Triffin of Yale University. In brief, he would have nations transfer part of their monetary reserves from holdings in dollars and pounds and put them into the International Monetary Fund.

The fund would become a sort of world central bank, just as nations now have their own domestic central banks.

Gold might or might not continue to play a key role in a new system.

While much study would be required before a new system could be worked out and agreed upon, it now seems clear that some of the key nations of Europe are at least willing to listen to ideas for a change.

*   *   *

In the United States. I am putting the finishing touches to this Postscript on the very day on which a new and dynamic President, surrounded by an unprecedently able Administrative team, is being inaugurated in Washington. While no decision could have been reached yet on the momentous issues discussed above, there can be doubt about the determination of the Kennedy Administration to study the problem in all its complex ramifications—political, as well as economic and financial—but in a bold and forward-looking spirit.

Such seemed to be also the mood of the Joint Economic Committee of Congress before which I was kindly called again to testify, on December 8, 1960. Interested readers may turn to the *Hearings* of that day's session for a full record of my presentation to the Committee and of the lively, but extremely sympathetic, debate that followed. Let me merely quote the concluding portion of my statement:

A fundamental reform of the international monetary system has long been overdue. Its necessity and urgency are further highlighted today by the imminent threat to the once mighty U.S. dollar. Both problems are closely intertwined and should be attacked together.

The first, and most feasible, action which could be taken would be to allow the International Monetary Fund to accept reserve deposits from its member central banks, just as our Federal Reserve System accepts reserve deposits from commercial member banks in this country. Under the rules of the Fund, such deposits would carry a gold-exchange guarantee making them extremely attractive to central banks and providing them with an alternative to the cashing of their present dollar balances in gold metal at the U.S. Treasury. About half of our short-term debt abroad could, as a result, be transferred from their present owners to the Fund, and cease to be a constant threat to our freedom of action with respect to both our domestic monetary management and the conduct of our foreign economic policy.

This suggestion could be implemented all the more rapidly as it has already received, in England, the unanimous blessing of the Radcliffe Committee on the Working of the Monetary System.

Its adoption would give us time to explore and negotiate with other interested countries the longer run reforms of the International Monetary Fund Charter necessary to provide our world with a stable and viable international monetary system, adjusted to the needs of our times.*

Conclusion. It would be foolhardy, of course, to imagine that such radical reforms as those advocated in this volume could ever be negotiated and implemented in the exact form in which they are presented here.

---

* *Hearings* of the Joint Economic Committee of Congress on the *Current Economic Situation and Short-Run Outlook*, Washington, 1961, p. 233.

One of the most complex aspects of this proposed reconstruction of our international monetary system is the manner in which operating functions and responsibilities will be distributed between world-wide organs of power—i.e. in this · case, the International Monetary Fund—and regional groupings, particularly the new Organization for Economic Cooperation and Development (OECD) and the European Economic Community (EEC). The need for decentralizing the vast responsibilities which the reforms proposed here would otherwise place on the IMF alone were stressed in my original articles for the *Banca Nazionale del Lavoro Quarterly Review*† and in my previous volume on *Europe and the Money Muddle*.‡

The need for such a multipronged approach has been made even more apparent to me by recent discussions of the various proposals made in this book. The most plausible objections presented against them are essentially political, rather than economic or financial, in nature. Major reserve holders, for instance, express doubts about relinquishing to the cumbersome and heterogeneous administrative machinery of the IMF full control over the large resources which a single, centralized and world-wide, deposit system would entrust to that institution. At the other end of the spectrum, the central banking leaders of EEC strenuously resist any unilateral move toward a European Community Reserve Fund (see pages 138–141 above), in the mistaken belief that the setting up of such a Fund might loosen present and vital links between their currencies, on the one hand, and the pound sterling and the dollar, on the other.

Both sets of fears might be allayed if the proposed IMF and EEC reforms were coupled with parallel action within the framework of the new OECD, grouping the Western European countries with the United States and Canada. This would entail the entrance of the latter two countries into the European Monetary Agreement, together with a considerable revamping and strengthening of that Agreement along the lines suggested in pages 121–130 of this book.

No purpose could be served by further crystal-gazing into the problem at this particular juncture. By the time this volume leaves the hands of the printer for those of my readers—several months from now—any prophecies that I might venture today will have be-

---

† See particularly pp. 120 and 128–131 above.
‡ See particularly pp. 257–266 and 302–304.

come part of history, or—far more probably—will have been discarded by it, or twisted out of any possible recognition or similarity with the dreams of a lone professor, peering dimly at the world through the stained glass windows of his ivory tower.

7. The Shape of Things to Come?

The following article, published by the London *Economist* in its Christmas issue of December 24, 1960 (pages 1325–1326) may appropriately bring this unfinished story to a futuristic close.

WHERE THE RAINBOW ENDED

By a deft stroke, The Economist *has got hold of the memoirs of Dr Per Jacobsson ten years before they are written. Chapter four, "The Brainwave of 1961," has a certain topical interest.*

IT WAS, in the words of that firm exponent of stable money, the Duke of Wellington, a damned close run thing. Speculation against the dollar, momentarily quietened by President Kennedy's inauguration, flared up suddenly again in March. The main cause seems to have been the bid made by General Motors for British Motor Corporation, to which the United Kingdom government gave its approval on condition that the bid be deemed to cover British Railways as well. This was fine for Britain, but it pushed the United States gold reserves below $16,000 million, and the fact that no more than two-fifths of the world's gold was buried under the United States naturally shook everyone's confidence in the stability of dollar prices.

Soon the pressure proved too much for the loose understanding that had been reached about management of the London gold market. The dollar price of gold shot up and on April 1st was quoted at $49. This time it could not so easily be brought back under control. Investors the world over, disillusioned with dividend cuts on their growth stocks, reverted to more ancient habits, and bought gold.

Plainly something had to be done. The economists, rising to the occasion, called a world conference in Fiji to thrash the matter out. After meeting all through the Easter vacation they issued a considered statement of 10,000 words which pointed out that fundamentally there was no problem. In a closely argued minority report, Sir Ralph Hawtrey identified the trouble to the undervaluation of sterling in 1949.

Still the exchange and bullion markets seethed. Samuel Montagu opened a recruiting office in Coventry. In June the directors of the

International Monetary Fund unanimously agreed that there should be no annual meeting that autumn. The markets heaved a sigh of relief. Soon after, however, an eavesdropper to a meeting of the National Temperance Council at Haywards Heath, England, reported a mystifying discussion about par values and fundamental disequilibrium. Worst suspicions were confirmed when it was found that fifteen Professor Skinners had registered at the Station Hotel.

So it appeared, that bleak and rainy summer, as though the world's currencies would after all have to succumb. The world's best economic brains, its most eminent practical bankers, had thought hard and long; but none had found a means of breaking the speculators' grip. More and more of them, privately, were beginning to think that the only way of getting rid of the speculators was to give in to them. The dons, back with their Fiji tans, were turning over the problem that had eluded them to their students. "Explain in 500 words what you consider to be the best means of checking the present flight from the dollar into gold." It livened up the seminars. But by one of those strange strokes of coincidence that go to the making of history, the paper of one of the students, a certain Joe Plain, did very much more.

It all happened because Mr. Plain discussed his paper one evening with his father, a principal in overseas finance at the Treasury. For two days Mr. Plain senior did nothing. Then, in the most tentative way, he passed up a memorandum to his assistant secretary. In the ordinary course of events, I have no doubt, matters would have stopped there. But this assistant secretary happened to be an old pupil of Professor J. K. Galbraith, now chairman of the Federal Reserve Board; and he felt it permissible, on an academic rather than an official level, to pass on to his old teacher the academic musings of his junior's no doubt unworldly but ingeniously minded son. On Friday, July 7th, he airmailed a copy of the paper to the professor's home address.

Who will ever forget the Monday that followed? It came as a thunderbolt not only to the public at large but to the whole financial community, from Treasury officials to central bankers. It came in the form of a short statement by the Federal Reserve Bank of New York, acting as agent for the U.S. Treasury.

In recent months doubts have been thrown on the continuance of the policy of the Federal Reserve in buying and selling gold at the parity of $35 an ounce, on the ground that market forces are inexorably pressing towards a higher price. The Federal Reserve has no wish to hold back the forces of the market. Forthwith, therefore, its undertaking to buy and sell gold at $35 an ounce, or at any other price, lapses.

In three sentences, the Fed had demonetised gold. The financial markets were knocked dizzy. The event was too large for men to take in. As they began working it out, they fastened on another statement which on my own initiative I put out for the International Monetary Fund:

The Federal Reserve Bank of New York announced today that it is ending its undertaking to sell gold to central banks at $35.08¾ and buy gold from any source at $34.91¼. The Fund approves this step. As an interim arrangement, until December 31, 1961, the Fund is taking over the commitments of the Federal Reserve, with certain differences. It will buy gold, at $35 less commission, only from central banks of its member countries, who will receive in return deposits with the Fund which can be used for all international payments; and it will be happy to sell gold at $35 plus commission to anyone. It assumes no obligation to buy gold after December 31st.

So, as the City editors quickly explained, anybody who held gold had better sell it quickly. For six months gold still had a value near $35, provided one's national central bank agreed to act as intermediary between the public and the International Monetary Fund. From the new year on, gold would be just a commodity, and busy calls went round to try to establish just what, as a commodity, gold would be worth.

Not everyone was happy with the discovery. The Zurich nursing homes had to open emergency wards: "It is the shock, the shock" the harassed doctors were heard to mutter. Kuwait decided to postpone its new retirement pension plan for all Arabs anywhere. Other countries saw their problems solved. In India the peasants were already carrying their gold into the banks; within three days the finance minister announced that the Indian government now had sufficient reserves at the IMF to dispense with all external aid for the third year plan. The Bank of France, too, enjoyed a windfall from its own people, and General de Gaulle's first impulse to make a proper hydrogen bomb gave way to a grand plan for full integration with Algeria at the French scale of social services, accepted by the Muslims by popular acclaim.

There were of course certain problems. South Africa was thunderstruck by the ruthless devaluation of its most important export commodity; it would not object to selling all its gold to the Fund but could not possibly dig it all out of the Rand in six months. The Fund offered special arrangements, the only condition being that South Africa should abolish *apartheid;* and after a bloodless *coup d'état* South Africa gratefully accepted. The other hard-hit gold producer, Russia, chewed over the problem a little longer. Here the Fund was asking simply that Russia should become a member and, in accordance with Article VIII, end all restrictions on current payments. The Old Guard fought passionately against; but Mr. Khrushchev—"Are we going to let the capitalists rob us of the value of our tens of billions of hard-dug gold?"—prevailed, and announced the decision on the same day as the cession of one thousand square miles of Mongolian desert to China. Most dramatically of all, even Switzerland decided to break with all precedent and join the Fund, though two cantons preferred to set up their own central banks; since the gold in their balance sheets has no ascertainable value it is to this day recorded in ounces.

This revolution in international finance of course transformed at one stroke the status of the International Monetary Fund. "The Fund," one commentator wrote, "now stands to the central banks of its member countries as does the Federal Reserve Board to its member banks." Possibly this was somewhat premature. At any rate the Fund secured a new hold on the public mind. In the vernacular, there was a rush to jump on the bandwagon. In response to strong pressure, I myself agreed to serve a second term as chairman and managing director. And recently we have been fortunate enough to persuade Lord Cromer to give up his promising start as governor of the Bank of England to return to his old and now highly coveted post as executive director of the Fund.

We have of course outgrown our new building, and at an early stage it was thought appropriate to move west, to a splendid new glass structure built over Fort Knox. In the early days visiting finance ministers were comforted by the sight of the bars of gold on which, as they still saw it, the security of their IMF deposits rested.

But such out-moded thinking soon lost sway, and when at a recent annual meeting the governor for the United Kingdom, under pressure at home to economise in his budget, pointed out that no less than $2.50 an ounce for gold could be obtained from dentists, the meeting decided there and then to put the whole lot out for public tender; a running income was assured by leasing Fort Knox to a grateful U.S. Defence Department for underground nuclear tests. The base of world liquidity at last broke free from its golden chain, and was determined instead by the hydraulic calculations provided free of charge by Professor Kendall of the London School of Economics.

So the operation that may well have saved the economy of the western world was brought to its triumphant conclusion. For the student of affairs, it brings two striking lessons. The first concerns the means by which the change was brought about. I well remember how the governor of a European central bank, who must be nameless, told me a few years ago that much the same scheme had been suggested by one of the less experienced delegates at that Haywards Heath gathering. "And what happened? It was laughed out of court." The central banks would refuse to co-operate; they would hang on to gold, which history had endowed with value, rather than part with it in exchange for a typewritten entry in the books of IMF. So much for the view of the men of the world, for whom money was a fixed and unchanging thing.

Yet just in those years Professor Sayers and the Radcliffe committee in England had reminded the public that money was whatever the public chose to accept as such. The same is true internationally. That is my second lesson. To those who doubt this, to those who feel that positive control over the course of economic events must for some reason stop short at the terms of international exchange, I need only say: remember The Year We Demonetised Gold.

P.P.S.: Since the Inauguration
(Written February 27, 1961)

President Kennedy's *Message to Congress on the Balance of Payments and Gold* (February 6, 1961) contrasted refreshingly with the drift and panic of previous official pronouncements and policies.

It emphasized the sharp deterioration of our *basic* balance in 1959, but also its recovery to "manageable proportions" in 1960. While reaffirming the need to bring these basic deficits to an end, and outlining a comprehensive program of action designed to achieve this objective within a reasonable time, the Message also diagnosed for the first time the role of short-term capital movements, and of the defects of the international monetary system itself, in the gold and dollar crisis which the free world has to face and to solve.

> Increasing international monetary reserves will be required to support the ever-growing volume of trade, services and capital movements among the countries of the free world. Until now, the free nations have relied upon increased gold production and continued growth in holdings of dollars and pounds sterling. In the future, it may not always be desirable or appropriate to rely entirely on these sources. We must now, in cooperation with other lending countries, begin to consider ways in which international monetary institutions—especially the International Monetary Fund—can be strengthened and more effectively utilized, both in furnishing needed increases in reserves, and in providing the flexibility required to support a healthy and growing world economy. I am therefore directing that studies to this end be initiated promptly by the Secretary of the Treasury.

The role which OECD might play, jointly with the IMF, in the restructuration of the international monetary and financial system was also foreshadowed in several other passages of the message:

> The United States must take the lead in harmonizing the financial and economic policies for growth and stability of those industrialized nations of the world whose economic behavior

179

significantly influences the course of the world economy and the trend of international payments.

And, later on:

> I earnestly request early action by the Senate approving United States membership in the Organization for Economic Cooperation and Development. The OECD, in which the industrialized countries of Western Europe, the United States and Canada will be joined, is of vital importance for assisting, on a cooperative basis, the developing countries of the free world. It will also provide a solid framework within which we can carry out intensive and frequent international consultations on the financial and monetary policies which must be pursued in order to achieve and maintain better balance in the international payments position.

A *United States Aide Mémoire on the Balance of Payments Situation,* released on February 20, amplified this point by stating in unusually forceful language:

> We are on the eve of creating a new phase in the history of the North Atlantic Alliance. We have new tasks; and the recovery of Western Europe in the 1950's has given us new resources. Together, the resources which we dispose are much larger than those we could command in the immediate post-war years and they are better distributed among us.
>
> To deal with these new tasks, we must begin by recognizing that we are interdependent in all we do; and that our common burdens must be shared in a way that our people will recognize as fair . . .
>
> In addition, we must all come to recognize a principle on which the United States has acted in the years after the Second World War. That principle is that a sustained accumulation of gold and other international reserves by any one country is disruptive to the international community. Especially now, when trade is expanding faster than gold production, we must learn to use our reserves on a communal basis, recognizing that one nation's gain can only be another nation's loss.
>
> It is in the light of these principles that the Government of the United States views the specific matter in hand; that is, the imbalance which has developed in the international payments

situation of the Free World. The present situation is marked
by a persistent basic deficit of some countries and a persistent
basic surplus of other countries. This had led to a substantial
increase in foreign liquid dollar holdings and, in recent years,
to an outflow of gold from the United States which has resulted
in a reduction of United States reserves. . .

Our common task is to design a reserves policy for the alliance
which will recognize the responsibilities to the common interest
of surplus and deficit nations alike . . .

These are brave new words. They now await implementation by
other countries as well as by us. Their exploration at the international level was officially, even though quietly and informally,
launched a few days ago with an invitation of Per Jacobsson to the
Executive Board of the International Monetary Fund to examine
possible changes in IMF policy and procedures.

That substantial progress will emerge from these discussions seems
to me a near certainty. The main question is whether the decisions
arrived at will open, or close, the door to the further adjustments
and historical evolution of our international monetary system indispensable to its survival and progress in a fast-changing world.

THE YALE PAPERBOUNDS